dynamic

HTML

The HTML Developer's Guide

JEFF RULE

ADDISON–WESLEY
An imprint of Addison Wesley Longman, Inc.

Reading, Massachusetts • Harlow, England • Menlo Park, California
Berkeley, California • Don Mills, Ontario • Sydney
Bonn • Amsterdam • Tokyo • Mexico City

The publisher offers discounts on this book when ordered in quantity for special sales. For more information, please contact:

AWL Direct Sales
Addison Wesley Longman, Inc.
One Jacob Way
Reading, Massachusetts 01867
(781) 944-3700

Visit AW on the Web: www.awl.com/cseng/

Library of Congress Cataloging-in-Publication Data

Rule, Jeff, 1968–
      Dynamic HTML : the HTML developer's guide / Jeff Rule.
            p.   cm.
      Includes index.
      ISBN 0-201-37961-9
      1. DHTML (Document markup language)   I. Title.
QA76.76.H94R85   1998
005.7'2—dc21   98–38784
                                                          CIP

ISBN 0-201-37961-9
Text printed on recycled and acid-free paper.
1 2 3 4 5 6 7 8 9 10—CRS—0201009998
First printing, November 1998

Special thanks to my parents,
Bruce and Jane,
for buying me my first computer,
an Apple IIe.

contents

FOR WHOM IS THIS BOOK INTENDED?

This book is written for the HTML developer who is trying to make the leap into Dynamic HTML and JavaScript. Let's face it, you can't do HTML forever, now that virtually every kid coming out of college has his or her own web page and knows HTML. You need to make the next step in web development—and Dynamic HTML is it.

Dynamic HTML: The HTML Developer's Guide is designed for the people that do the grunt work of web development. These individuals take graphics from the art department and text from the editors and then work magic with tables to achieve the right appearance. They update Internet sites and intranet sites. Caffeine and stress are key ingredients in their lives. Their nontechnical bosses can't seem to figure out why it's so hard to put up a page, because "After all, the graphics and words are already done!" These bosses want a cool pop-out menu that they saw on the Discovery Channel site or the flying logo they saw when their kids were at the Disney site last night.

This book is for the oppressed masses, who cry out for an example they can take apart and understand! It provides Dynamic HTML demos that are explained in clear, no-nonsense language.

WHAT IS DYNAMIC HTML?

You've heard about Dynamic HTML. It's the buzzword of the day all over the web. But what is it? Is it a series of new extensions to HTML? Is it JavaScript? VBScript? JScript? ECMAScript? Cascading Style Sheets (CSS)? In fact, Dynamic HTML is a catch-all phrase for all of these technologies and the way that they work together.

The version 4.0 browsers from Netscape and Microsoft that support Dynamic HTML incorporate some new HTML tags from HTML 4.0. They also support CSS and an upgraded version of JavaScript. All these elements work together to make up Dynamic HTML. Think of it this way: CSS gives you pixel-perfect control of where your text and graphics go. If you want a graphic's upper-left corner to be 100 pixels from the left side of the screen and 200 pixels from the top of the screen, you can use CSS to put it there. CSS replaces tables as the new way to lay out your page. JavaScript (and VBScript in Internet Explorer 4) are the scripting languages that help you move things around the screen or change graphics. JavaScript is what puts the "dynamic" in Dynamic HTML.

WHO AM I?

My name is Jeff Rule, and I work at Discovery Channel Online (http://www.discovery.com), which is the online presence of the Discovery Channel cable network. Discovery is a top-40 content web site developed in Bethesda, Maryland. I began working in CD-ROM development back in 1993 by doing CD-ROM projects and computer-based training (CBT), mainly in Macromedia's Authorware and Director products. I'd also done some basic HTML. When Shockwave first emerged, however, I really got interested in the web.

At Discovery I'm in charge of Dynamic HTML and other high-end web multimedia development, such as Shockwave. I also look at "bleeding-edge" technology, which is how I first encountered Dynamic HTML. But it's not bleeding-edge technology anymore, I promise!

COMPANION WEB SITE

The companion web site for this book is DHTML Demos, located at http://www.ruleweb.com/dhtml/index.html. I started this site back in September 1997 as a source of Internet Explorer 4.0 demos. Later, as I gained a better understanding of the differing document object models (DOM), I began creating Netscape-compatible demos. The site originated as a showcase for the Dynamic HTML work I was doing at Discovery Channel, allowing our editors to see some of the possibilities of Dynamic HTML and its possible applications for the stories we were working on. It later escaped to the web and now makes its home at RuleWeb, my development company.

Since its inception, the site has grown substantially. Today, it is one of the more trafficked Dynamic HTML sites on the web. At the site you will find the demos referenced in this book as well as additional demos. Look to this site for code, working examples, and for the latest information on the emerging field of DHTML.

PHILOSOPHY OF THIS BOOK

I learned HTML and JavaScript by taking apart other people's examples and then experimenting with the code until I figured out what it did. Not surprisingly, it was a time-consuming process. When I started the DHTML Demos site, I wanted to offer lots of demonstrations that people could also take apart and understand. I created the demonstrations as much for myself as for the development community. The demos were components that I could plug into a story I was developing for Discovery, without having to write the code from scratch every time. If I needed a pop-out menu, for example, I already had one written.

The site continued to grow and I received lots of questions about the demonstrations, but I didn't have time to respond to even a fraction of the messages I received. This book is an attempt to explain those demonstrations in detail and take the code apart, line by line. This method will help you, the developer, to use this code in your own pages. At the same time, you will understand it enough that you can modify the code and create new scripts. (Because some terms may be new to you, I have included a glossary at the back of the book. Terms defined in the glossary are set in bold in the text.)

If there is one thing I believe in on the web, it's the **VIEW SOURCE** command. I hope this book goes even further in explaining the code you see in your View Source window.

WHAT YOU'LL NEED TO USE THIS BOOK

You'll need:

- An HTML editor (I prefer Allaire Homesite for PC or BBEdit for Macintosh)
- Netscape Communicator 4.x or 5.x
- Microsoft Internet Explorer 4.x or 5.x

These browsers are currently the only ones in which Dynamic HTML works.

ACKNOWLEDGMENTS

I would like to acknowledge the tremendous help of Joe Halladay in creating the cover art for this book. I wish my sister, Kristin Rule, the best of luck as she prepares to enter web development. With luck, she'll avoid all the mistakes I've made.

I would also like to thank Terry Veit, Todd Baldwin, and the rest of Discovery Channel Online's design staff for their feedback. Special thanks to John Hulson and the rest of the digital lab for taking a chance on me and making me feel welcome; and John Bell, for allowing me to push the edge of web multimedia.

foreword

I volunteered to write this foreword because Jeff Rule's book is the best text I've read on the subject of Dynamic HTML. As the web moves closer to a multimedia experience, publishers will have to grasp many new concepts, tools, and methodologies—all of which this book describes in great detail. Because so much hype exists in this particular area of web development, it's really important to get straight facts and advice from someone who is an actual practitioner of this craft.

Throughout this book, Jeff references Dynamic HTML projects he has produced for Discovery Online, which gives this book a real-world perspective that other books on this subject don't share. He knows his stuff, and knows the pitfalls, problems, and solutions from first-hand experiences. His descriptions of JavaScript, Cascading Style Sheets, DOM, ActiveX, and plug-ins are easy to understand because he references his own experiences using these techniques. He's not afraid to say when something doesn't work correctly, or warn you not to use a bell or whistle. The honesty in this book is truly rare and refreshing.

As an author, I value another author's ability to write in an accessible manner that makes difficult concepts easier to understand, rather than more complex. Too many web books either talk down to their audience or overwhelm them with too much technical detail. This book is the perfect blend of conversational tone, solid technical explanations, personal insights, and valuable exercises. Jeff's tone is genuine throughout; it is obvious to me that Dynamic HTML is a subject of great personal interest and passion to him.

If you want to wrap your head around the newest direction the web is taking, then this book will help you grasp Dynamic HTML concepts, potential benefits, and problems. It's an enjoyable read and contains a wealth of helpful tricks and tips. After reading Jeff's book, you will be able to implement the scripts and ideas in your own web site, or at least be able to make more informed decisions about which new directions to embrace and which to discard. This book will be helpful to many types of web publishers, whether you're in the trenches writing code, directing others to write it for you, or just seeking information on the latest leading (and bleeding) edge web technology.

A true expert—someone with real-world experience in a subject this new and important—is worth their weight in gold. These pages are laden with value well beyond the cost of the book. I hope you enjoy it as much as I did!

> —Lynda Weinman
> Web design author and educator
> http://www.lynda.com

chapter 1

INTRODUCTION

WHAT WE'LL COVER
- **Scripting languages**
- **Standards**
- **Future browsers**
- **Browser compatibility**
- **Creating compatibility**

Taking apart other people's work is the best way to learn, especially when the developer is there to give you pointers and explain the code. That's what this book is all about. If you'd like to dive directly into the examples, jump to Chapter 3 and we'll discuss Cascading Style Sheets (CSS). In this first chapter, we'll discuss some background information about Dynamic HTML.

If you've looked at Dynamic HTML books or programming books in general, you'll notice that the author typically makes you read through a hundred or so pages of information about object models, syntax, and variables before you ever see an example. These examples are often so rudimentary that they're of no use on real-world web pages.

When you first picked up HTML, you probably didn't learn it in that way. You may have purchased a reference book to look up what certain tags meant. But you most likely looked at other people's work or examined examples created by other people working on your site. Very few programmers sat down, read a book, and knew HTML after finishing the text.

In this book, we'll take a hands-on approach to learning Dynamic HTML. We'll look at a variety of demonstrations and then take the code apart, line by line. You can then extend your knowledge to write new scripts.

THE FUTURE OF WEB CONTENT

Page- Versus Stage-Based Content

Before the version 4.0 browsers became available, web-based content was restricted to page-based content. That is, pages loaded and remained static. Although some pages might include interactive Shockwave content or a streaming movie, in general web pages behaved much like book pages. You proceeded from page to page to access new content. The introduction of Dynamic HTML in Netscape Communicator 4.0 allowed objects on the screen to be hidden and shown. It also allowed events to occur over time. Thus characters could be introduced and then leave after carrying out an action. The web page became a stage. In this way, Dynamic HTML returned much of the functionality offered by multimedia design tools.

The release of Netscape Communicator 4.0 was the first step in making web development more like CD-ROM development. The new browsers include new DOMs, and will allow developers to create time-based content that involves interactive story telling. Remember interactive TV, which died a few years ago? That's what web development will grow up to be.

SCRIPTING LANGUAGES

A Brief Introduction to JavaScript Syntax

Scripting languages are bits of code that are included in the HTML of a document. They are separated from the HTML by script tags such as the following:

```
<script language="JavaScript">
<!--code is inserted here-->
</script>
```

We will often call JavaScript functions. Functions are bits of JavaScript code that cause something to happen on the page. For example, they might trigger an animation, update the time, grab information about the user's browser, or grab the coordinates of a mouse click. For now, you simply need to recognize what they look like. Here is an example:

```
function init() {
        //insert function here
}
```

This function is called **init**. If you started this function, it would trigger the code contained inside the **{}**. Functions can be given any name you like. I generally try to use descriptive names. If the function will make a menu pop out from the left side of the screen, for example, I'd call it **popout**. The brackets following the function name are used to pass parameters to the function. We'll see examples of this procedure later. Notice that the double slashes (**//**) are a method of inserting comments in your JavaScript code; they are used in the same way that **<!-- -->** is used in HTML.

Scripting languages like JavaScript and **programming languages** like Java differ in that Java is compiled into an applet before it is downloaded. "Compiling the code" means that the original code written by the programmer is translated into machine code that the computer can read more easily. Once compiled, no changes can be made to the code. If the original code is modified, it must be recompiled.

JavaScript is an interpreted language. In other words, the browser looks at the code and translates it to the computer in real time. JavaScript has to be "predigested" in advance for the computer. As a result, programs written in this language should run more slowly than Java programs. Because JavaScript programs are usually small and don't need to be loaded like Java, however, they actually run much faster than Java.

Other Scripting/Programming Languages

You may be somewhat confused by the number of scripting and programming languages that are available on the web. Let's look at some of the more common ones.

JavaScript: **JavaScript** is the original scripting language. It was first included in Netscape Navigator 2.0.

JScript: JScript is a clone of JavaScript that was originally introduced by Microsoft when Netscape refused to license JavaScript. It was reverse-engineered from JavaScript and first introduced in Internet Explorer 3.0. The reverse engineering was not very successful, however, and many conflicts existed between JScript and JavaScript in the Netscape 3 and Internet Explorer 3 browsers. Version 4 of both browsers is much more compatible.

ECMAScript: This general-purpose, cross-platform programming language is derived from JavaScript. Netscape turned over control of JavaScript to the European Computer Manufacturers Association (ECMA), an international industry association dedicated to the standardization of information and communication systems, in an effort to transform the language into a universal standard. We'll discuss ECMAScript later in this chapter.

VBScript: **VBScript** is a stripped-down version of Visual Basic that replicates much of the functionality of JavaScript. It works only with Internet Explorer.

Active X: **Active X** components are now part of Microsoft's Component Object Model (COM) for distributed applications. Today you will see them on the web as small programs that run in the browser window. In some cases, they provide functionality similar to that offered by plug-ins. In other cases, they add functionality to the browser by tying into Windows architectures such as Direct X.

Almost all of the demos included in this book are written in JavaScript. Occasionally VBScript is used for some examples that work only in Internet Explorer. Although ECMAScript is now the approved standard, both Netscape and Microsoft continue to add their own extensions to JavaScript and JScript, respectively. As a result, ECMAScript will continue to lag behind the current versions of these two languages.

You also may have heard of **XML** (**Extensible Markup Language**), which is the universal format for data placed on the web. XML allows developers to describe and deliver structured data from any application in a standard, consistent way. This language does not replace HTML; instead, it is a complementary format.

The World Wide Web Consortium (W3C), a web standards committee, which finalized the standard in February 1998, calls XML "a common syntax for expressing structure in data." "Structured data" refers to data that are tagged because of their content, meaning, or use. XML is used to explicitly identify the information in the tag. For example, in HTML the **`<h2>`** tag describes the size of the text inside the tag. In XML you define your own tags that explicitly identify the kind of information in the tag, such as **`<price>`** or **`<upc code>`**. The appearance of the information, such as its font size, is then defined separately in the CSSs (which we'll discuss in Chapter 3).

Consider another example. When data is delivered in XML from a web server and stored on the client, the user can change the data locally and present it dynamically. In contrast, HTML describes how to present hyperlinked pages on the screen. Essentially, information is static in HTML and unavailable for manipulation. By delivering the data separately from the HTML structure, the user can change and manipulate the data. A real-world example might involve the receipt of information about ten items including name, manufacturer, color, and price. You could change the data so that it lists the items in alphabetical order, or from lowest price to most expensive. You could perform this operation without assistance from the server. As a result, you don't have to send a request back across the web to a database every time you want to see the data in a different format.

XML can also be used to create new languages. Microsoft's **Channel Definition Format (CDF)** is such a language that is written in XML. Microsoft's Internet Explorer 4.0 browser contains a parser, which understands the special tags that are used in CDF, such as **<ABSTRACT>**. When new tags are created, the parser must understand them and tell the browser how to present them on the screen.

Because of its adaptable nature, XML will be in wide use on the Internet in coming years.

STANDARDS

Table 1-1 lists the standards currently in use on the web.

TABLE 1-1. WEB STANDARDS

Standard	Meaning	Organization
ECMAScript	Scripting language based on JavaScript	ECMA
HTML 4.0	Hypertext Markup Language	W3C
CSS1 and CSS2	Cascading Style Sheets (Levels 1 and 2)	W3C
CSS-P	Cascading Style Sheets—Positioning	W3C
XML	Extensible Markup Language	W3C
DOM	Document Object Model—three parts	W3C

Desperately Seeking Standards

You may have noticed that almost nothing on the web is standardized. Dynamic HTML in Netscape Communicator 4 and Internet Explorer 4 work differently. JavaScript works differently in every browser. Even the Macintosh and PC versions of the same browser work differently. Why is this so? Because standards take a long time to develop. Standards committees are constrained by the fact that they must get the standard right the first time. They can't afford to experiment. On the other hand, Microsoft and Netscape are businesses. If they both introduced browsers based on standards, then they would be selling the same browser—and neither company would have a competitive advantage. Consequently, both frequently develop new features that are incompatible with other competing browsers. They hope that the features will be popular and accepted into the next round of standards. Some of the "innovations" never make it to the standards. Remember "background sound" in Internet Explorer? Or layers in Netscape Communicator 4? Layers were another innovation that was turned down by the W3C when it decided on standards for CSS? Despite the inconvenience of the incompatibilities, we must remember that there would be no innovation if the browser companies didn't try new things.

COMPATIBILITY

Dynamic HTML (DHTML) consists of four components:

- HTML
- Cascading style sheets
- A scripting language
- Document Object Model (DOM)

These components work together to produce the collective technique called **Dynamic HTML**. We'll talk about them in order from most compatible to least compatible.

HTML Compatibility

Internet Explorer 4 and Netscape 4 both support **HTML** 4.0, a standard created by W3C. Both of these browsers also support older, proprietary tags so as to provide backward compatibility. Very few tags have ever been completely "deprecated," which is browser terminology for "removed" or "no longer supported."

You may wonder how an HTML standard relates to scripting and DHTML. Because DHTML must control HTML objects (such as pictures and text), it must be able to interact with HTML. To allow this interaction, HTML 4.0 formalizes the inclusion of the **<script>** and **<noscript>** tags. These tags allow a scripting language to be used within the HTML page and have been employed since the introduction of Netscape Navigator 2.0. HTML 4.0 also takes into account the Event Model. Events are actions that the user takes, such as loading a page, moving the mouse, or clicking on the screen. The Event Model controls how the user's actions trigger JavaScript functions.

HTML 4.0 has been designed to be language neutral. That is, it can interact with JavaScript, JScript, VBScript, ECMAScript, and any other scripting language that might come along in the future.

Style Sheets (CSS) Compatibility

CSSs are relatively browser neutral. That is, they work equally well in many different browsers, including Netscape Communicator 4 and Internet Explorer 4. These two browsers support the majority of CSS1 (Level 1), the standard published by W3C.

Style sheets were created in an effort to separate layout from content. Separating form and content in this way is a good idea. It facilitates maintenance and, when combined with scripting, it allows the user to apply several different layouts to the same data by changing style sheets.

Style sheets control alignment, font faces, and text color. In fact, the HTML 4.0 standard drops such familiar tags as **<font>**. Don't worry—the major browser manufacturers will continue to support these tags for years to come so as to maintain backward compatibility.

Style sheets are also used in a somewhat less browser-neutral standard: Cascading Style Sheet Positioning (CSS-P). In general, you can regard CSS and CSS-P as the same thing since it all ends up between the **<style>** tags. The major discrepancy between Internet Explorer 4 and Netscape 4 is the visibility attribute. As shown in Table 1-2, this attribute uses different values in the two browsers. As showing and hiding HTML objects is a major part of DHTML, these differing syntaxes hinder compatibility. We will discuss ways to create compatibility using object and browser detection later in this chapter.

TABLE 1-2. COMMON POSITION ATTRIBUTES

Attribute	Values
position	absolute | relative
left	Pixel position relative to outer element

continued

TABLE 1-2. COMMON POSITION ATTRIBUTES *(Continued)*

Attribute	Values
`top`	Pixel position relative to outer element
`visibility`	IE4 (`visible | hidden | inherit`)
	NS4 (`show | hide | inherit`)
`z-index`	Integer controlling position in stack

Another standard in the works is called CSS-2. We will discuss it in more detail when we examine CSS in Chapter 3.

Scripting Language Compatibility

ECMAScript-262: The Lowest Common Denominator

ECMAScript, or more properly ECMAScript-262, is the only universal scripting language on the web. As a result, it is important for Dynamic HTML programmers. ECMAScript was created by developers from Microsoft, Netscape, IBM, Sun Microsystems, Inprise (formerly Borland International), and other software companies with the help of the European Computer Manufacturers Association (ECMA). The group began its work in January 1997 and had a finished draft ready 10 months later— very fast for standards development. According to all reports, Netscape and Microsoft staff members worked very well together on the team.

The language is based on Netscape's JavaScript, with some modifications from Microsoft's JScript. You can think of ECMAScript as JavaScript 1.1 with the bugs fixed. Thus, Netscape Navigator 2 and Internet Explorer 3 (whose JavaScript implementation is based on Navigator 2) are not ECMAScript-compliant. Netscape used ECMAScript as the foundation when it built JavaScript 1.2, the scripting language for Netscape Communicator 4.0. Microsoft has also included ECMAScript as the basis for JScript 3.0, which is used in Internet Explorer 4.0.

Both Netscape and Microsoft extended their scripting languages beyond ECMAScript to include proprietary language. As noted earlier, standards committees tend to lag one browser version behind the browser manufacturers in implementing updates. By pushing ahead, the browser companies create new syntax that will serve as the basis for the next round of standards.

Scripters often forget an important distinction when they learn scripting for browsers. The scripting language is the syntax—the way things are written. The second part, the DOM, dictates how the written scripting language controls the elements on the screen, such as graphics and text. The core scripting language is covered under ECMAScript, but the DOM is a separate component. We'll discuss the DOM in detail in Chapter 2.

CREATING COMPATIBILITY

Creating compatible web pages becomes more difficult with each release of a new browser. Many users already have all the functionality they need in Netscape Navigator 2/3 or Internet Explorer 3, and are reluctant to upgrade. Developers must also consider the conflicting DOMs of the version 4 browsers as well as how the newer JavaScript code they write will look on older browsers. In addition, some people with newer browsers may turn off JavaScript for one reason or another. Creating compatibility is a combination of art, science, and, yes, luck. Several different techniques have been developed to deal with these incompatibilities.

BACKWARD COMPATIBILITY

Style Sheets

Style sheet information can be hidden from older browsers by surrounding them with comment tags, as shown below:

```
<style>
<!--
insert style info here
-->
</style>
```

HTML

The key to creating backward-compatible Dynamic HTML lies in how a browser deals with unfamiliar tags or attributes. According to the W3C HTML specifications, browsers should ignore any tags or attributes that they don't recognize. That is, unknown tags are simply skipped over. If an unknown attribute is found, the browser acts as if it had never existed, but continues to process the rest of the tags normally. This simple behavior creates options for laying out HTML that will have a reasonable appearance in browsers with differing levels of functionality.

Older browsers will ignore new tags such as **DIV** and **LAYER**, which play a large role in positioned content. The **DIV** tag is used in both Internet Explorer 4.0 and Netscape Communicator 4.0, allowing the user to create "divisions" on the page. The **LAYER** tag produces layers in Netscape Communicator 4.0 that are similar to **DIV** areas (discussed in more detail in Chapter 3). We can make use of this functionality to create pages that are acceptable in older browsers.

<NOLAYER> Tag

Netscape Communicator 4 includes a specific tag to help create Dynamic HTML that is compatible with older browsers, the **<NOLAYER>** tag. The **<NOLAYER>** tag enables you to add content to a page that will be displayed only in browsers that do not support the **<LAYER>** tag. Netscape Communicator 4.0 will ignore any content contained within the **<NOLAYER>** tag. As a result, you can include alternative content for older browsers in the same source page as Dynamic HTML content. The tag provides the equivalent functionality as **<NOFRAMES>** does for browsers that don't support frames.

The **LAYER** tag is useful if you have Dynamic HTML that occurs in one place on the page and can be replaced by an animated GIF or static graphic. Although Netscape 5 will still support this tag, its use will not be recommended. It will be largely replaced by the **DIV** tag.

<LAYER> and <IFRAME> Tags

Another technique works only in the version 4 browsers and also makes use of the fact that a browser ignores unfamiliar HTML. This technique is founded on the following premise:

- The **<LAYER>** tag is unique to Netscape 4 and is used to create floating layers of content.
- The **<IFRAME>** tag is unique to Internet Explorer 4 and allows a single frame to be placed anywhere on the page.

Alternative content for both browsers can be placed in these tags, and only the appropriate Dynamic HTML will be displayed. This script should be used in conjunction with a JavaScript browser detect, as Internet Explorer 3 will also display **<IFRAME>** material.

Listing 1-1 demonstrates the use of **<LAYER>** and **<IFRAME>** tags.

LISTING 1-1. <LAYER> AND <IFRAME> TAGS

```
<!-- layer tag for Netscape Communicator -->
<layer name="skeletonheadworksxTop" left="0" top="0" width="350"
height="400">
<layer name="skeletonheadworksxSub"
src="skeleton_ns.html"></layer>
</layer>

<!-- iframe tag for Microsoft Explorer 4.0 -->
<iframe name="skeletonheadworksx" src="skeleton_ie.html"
frameborder="0" noresize width="350" height="400"
marginwidth="0" marginheight="0" scrolling="no"></iframe>
```

The **<LAYER>** tag will display the file skeleton_ns.html in Netscape 4; the **<IFRAME>** tag will display skeleton_ie.html in Internet Explorer 4.

Script Versions

Another problem arises when older browsers try to execute scripting code that works only in a particular version 4 browser. Obviously, Netscape Navigator 2.0, which is JavaScript 1.0-compliant, will not be able to execute code written in JavaScript 1.2 from Netscape 4. By specifying the JavaScript version number in the script code, we can force older browsers to ignore code that they do not understand:

```
<SCRIPT LANGUAGE="JavaScript1.2">
```

Even though Internet Explorer 4 does not officially support JavaScript 1.2, it will still read the code in these tags. This browser officially supports JavaScript 1.1 plus JScript 3 extensions. Also note that no space separates the word "JavaScript" and the version number.

Alternative Pages Using Browser Detection

While this technique may initially seem to be highly labor-intensive, it is not always so. If you have only a few pages that are using Dynamic HTML, then it may be easier to create alternative pages for older browsers. This option may prove easier than debugging a page in three different browsers while trying to keep many **IF THEN** statements straight in your head. For a large-scale web site that is updated frequently, this method may become impractical; for a small site or pages that will be up for only a short time, this method may be simpler. For example, at Discovery Channel, I will sometimes create a multimedia element to one of our stories developed in Netscape Dynamic HTML, Internet Explorer 4 Dynamic HTML, and Java for older browsers. I will create three different pages that are identical except for the code underlying the multimedia. I will then perform a **browser detection**, either using JavaScript to pick the browser version or on the server. The user receives a seamless experience, depending on the browser he or she is using. Because these stories remain available for only a few weeks to a month, I almost never have to update them after their initial creation.

Listing 1-2 shows some sample code I've used to detect browsers.

LISTING 1-2. BROWSER DETECTION CODE (AVAILABLE AT
HTTP://WWW.RULEWEB.COM/INDEX.HTML)

```
1.  <HTML>
2.  <HEAD>
3.  <TITLE>Jeff Rule Home Browser Detect and Redirect</TITLE>
4.  <SCRIPT LANGUAGE = "JavaScript">

5.  bName = navigator.appName;
6.  bVer = parseInt(navigator.appVersion);

7.  if       (bName == "Netscape" && bVer == 4) ver = "n4";
8.  else if (bName == "Netscape" && bVer == 3) ver = "n3";
9.  else if (bName == "Netscape" && bVer == 2) ver = "n2";
10. else if (bName == "Microsoft Internet Explorer" && bVer == 4)
    ver = "e4";
11. else if (bName == "Microsoft Internet Explorer" && bVer == 3)
    ver = "e3";
12. else if (bName == "Microsoft Internet Explorer" && bVer == 2)
    ver = "e2";

13. if (ver == "n4") {
14. window.location.href="indexnetcaster.html"
15. }

16. if (ver == "n3") {
17. window.location.href="indexjava.html"
18. }
19. if (ver == "n2") {
20. window.location.href="indexjava.html"
21. }

22. if (ver == "e4") {
23. window.location.href="indexie4.html"
24. }
```

```
25. if (ver == "e3") {
26. window.location.href="indexjava.html"
27. }
28. if (ver == "e2") {
29. window.location.href="indexnojava.html"
30. }
31. </SCRIPT>
32. <BODY BGCOLOR = "#FFFFFF" TEXT = "#000000" LINK = "#B8860B"
    ALINK = "#8B0000" VLINK = "#B8860B">
33. <CENTER>
34. <center><h1>Browser Detection in Progress if there is an error
    connect with this <a
    href="indexnojava.html">link</a></h1></center>
35. </CENTER>
36. </BODY>
37. </HTML>
```

Although this code is very simple, it detects nearly all browsers in use today, including the following:

- Netscape Navigator 2
- Netscape Navigator 3
- Netscape Communicator 4
- Internet Explorer 2
- Internet Explorer 3
- Internet Explorer 4

Once a browser is detected, the user is sent to the appropriate page. Although we won't go through all the details of the code, let's follow how Netscape 4 is detected and redirected to a compatible page.

Lines 5–6:

```
5. bName = navigator.appName;
6. bVer = parseInt(navigator.appVersion);
```

The first line uses built-in methods to detect the application's name. In this case, it determines that the user is browsing with Netscape Navigator. (Note: The term **navigator** is used in the detection of both Netscape browsers and Internet Explorer.) The value is then assigned to the variable bName.

The next line detects the version number of the browser. In this case, we are pretending that the user is browsing with Netscape 4. Thus the version number "4" is assigned to the variable **bVer**.

Lines 7–12:

```
 7. if       (bName == "Netscape" && bVer == 4) ver = "n4";
 8. else if (bName == "Netscape" && bVer == 3) ver = "n3";
 9. else if (bName == "Netscape" && bVer == 2) ver = "n2";
10. else if (bName == "Microsoft Internet Explorer" && bVer == 4)
    ver = "e4";
11. else if (bName == "Microsoft Internet Explorer" && bVer == 3)
    ver = "e3";
12. else if (bName == "Microsoft Internet Explorer" && bVer == 2)
    ver = "e2";
```

Lines 7 through 12 present a series of **IF THEN** statements that would read in simple English as follows:

If the browser name is Netscape and the version number is 4 then set **ver** equal to **n4**.

The code then proceeds to detect any other browser with which the user might be surfing, and assigns it an appropriate value.

Lines 13–15:

```
13. if (ver == "n4") {
14. window.location.href="indexnetcaster.html"
15. }
```

These lines then take a look at **n4**, which represents both the browser name (Netscape) and the version number (4) and redirects the user to the appropriate page using `window.location.href`. In this case, we send the Netscape 4 user to a page that allows him or her to subscribe to the author's Netcaster channel.

The **BODY** of the HTML document also contains a link to a version of the home page that uses neither Java nor JavaScript. This link is placed in the body to accommodate browsers that are very old and do not have JavaScript and users who prefer to surf with this option turned off.

As you can see from the code, we have produced four separate home pages. One is for Netscape 4 users and provides a Netcaster channel and a Java menu, one is for Internet Explorer 4 users and provides Java and a CDF channel, one offers a Java menu for version 3 browsers and Netscape 2, and a final version handles Internet Explorer 2 users and others with JavaScript turned off.

This technique may seem like a lot of work, but sometimes it is also the best solution.

Alternative Scripts Using Object Detection

An alternative to browser detection is **object detection**. Object detection determines whether a browser will work with a certain object, such as **LAYER** or **IFRAME**. If the browser can support that object, then it uses the code. If it is unable to support the object, then it uses alternative code.

Consider the following scenario. You build some code in Internet Explorer 4 that rotates your logo in three dimensions while increasing stock prices and washing the boss's car. It's an amazing bit of code. You wish that other browsers could read the code and use this object, but they can't. You use browser detection to send all other browsers to a static page. Next month, Netscape 5 comes out; it supports this great code using your object. You must then rewrite the code to include Netscape 5. What a pain! If you'd used object detection, this problem never would have happened. Think of object detection as providing forward compatibility.

Listing 1-3 provides the relevant code.

LISTING 1-3. OBJECT DETECTION CODE

```
<script language="JavaScript1.2">
if (document.layers) {n=1;ie=0}
if (document.all) {n=0;ie=1}

function init() {
     if (n) {insert ns4 function here}
     if (ie) {insert ie4 function here}
}

</script>
```

You'll want to deal with two objects in Dynamic HTML: **document.layers** and **document.all**. The first tells you that you're dealing with Netscape 4.0, as it tests whether the layer object is present. The second tests whether you are using Internet Explorer 4's DOM. By using these two objects, you can present only information that can be properly displayed in the browser. Table 1-3 indicates which browsers support which objects.

TABLE 1-3. JAVASCRIPT OBJECT SUPPORT

	Netscape Navigator 2	Netscape Navigator 3	Netscape Navigator 4	Internet Explorer 3	Internet Explorer 4
Applets Display Java applets	No	Yes	Yes	Yes[1]	Yes[1]
Arrays Use arrays	No	Yes	Yes	Yes	Yes
Cascading Style Sheets Control CSS	No	No	Yes[2]	Yes[8]	Yes
Cookies Browser's cookie	Yes	Yes	Yes	Yes*	Yes
Date Time/date	Yes	Yes	Yes	Yes	Yes

continued

TABLE 1-3. JAVASCRIPT OBJECT SUPPORT *(Continued)*

	Netscape Navigator 2	Netscape Navigator 3	Netscape Navigator 4	Internet Explorer 3	Internet Explorer 4
Events Extra event information	No	No	Yes[3]	No	Yes[3]
External scripts SRC attribute	No	Yes	Yes	No[4]	Yes
Forms Submission forms	Yes	Yes	Yes	Yes*	Yes
Frames Control frames	Yes	Yes	Yes	Yes	Yes
Images Control images	No	Yes	Yes	No[5]	Yes
Java enabled Detect Java	No	Yes	Yes	No	Yes
Links Control links	Yes	Yes	Yes	Yes	Yes
Location Control location	Yes	Yes	Yes	Yes*	Yes
Navigator Browser information	Yes	Yes	Yes	Yes	Yes
mimeTypes mime types	No	Yes	Yes	No	No
Window Control window	Yes[5,6]	Yes[6]	Yes	Yes*,[5,6]	Yes[6]
Write Write HTML	Yes*	Yes*	Yes	Yes	Yes

*Implementation buggy or incomplete.
[1]Access to Active X as well, but no Java calls.
[2]Navigator allows only predisplay control and the display cannot be modified after it is written to the screen, except with positioning.
[3]The event model is different in Internet Explorer and Navigator.
[4]External scripts are supported in Internet Explorer 3.01, but not in version 3.0.
[5]scroll(), focus(), and blur() are not supported.
[6]moveTo(), moveBy(), resizeTo(), and resizeBy() are not supported.
[7]Internet Explorer 3 for Macintosh supports the image object.
[8]Very limited implementation.

LINKS

ECMAScript
http://www.ecma.ch/STAND/Ecma-262.htm

JavaScript
http://developer.netscape.com/tech/javascript/index.html

JScript
http://www.microsoft.com/scripting/default.htm?/scripting/jscript/default.htm

VBScript
http://www.microsoft.com/scripting/default.htm?/scripting/vbscript/default.htm

XML
http://www.w3c.org/XML/ and http://www.microsoft.com/XML/

W3C
http://www.w3c.org

Active X
http://www.microsoft.com/com/

THE DOCUMENT OBJECT MODEL (DOM)

When the W3C released the first draft of its Document Object Model specification, in October 1997, many observers commented that it looked an awful lot like Microsoft's DOM. Certainly the W3C DOM leans more toward Microsoft's atomized approach than toward Netscape's layer-based model.

—**D.C. Denison**, *Web Review*, December 5, 1997
http://webreview.com/wr/pub/97/12/05/dom/index.html

WHAT WE'LL COVER

- Netscape Communicator 4.0 DOM
- Microsoft Internet Explorer 4.0 DOM
- W3C's proposed DOM

Previous browsers had very limited **Document Object Models** (**DOMs**). It wasn't until the introduction of Netscape 3 that scripting could be used to implement such basic elements as dynamically changing graphics. Netscape 3 allowed scripters to perform button rollovers for the first time. A real conflict arose, however, when scripters noticed that these same scripts didn't work in Internet Explorer 3. Microsoft's browser didn't implement the Image element as a scriptable object. Thus attempts to adjust the *src* property of an image prompted a JavaScript error.

The DOM defines how HTML objects (such as graphics and text) are exposed to the scripting language. In other words, it controls how the scripting language is used to change attributes such as color or selection of a graphic image.

The document has become an application in which developers need to set up and manage objects. For its part, the web page has become an interface through which we interact with information. No longer is it just a static entity—instead, it now moves, changes, and rearranges itself. We use scripting to support these movements or actions, which are called "behaviors." The DOM is the backbone for these behaviors. This framework controls how the behaviors interact with the objects on the screen. It tells us how scripts reference objects, how styles are applied to elements, how scripts change styles, and how styles initiate scripts.

The DOM is a hierarchy (or a tree, if you prefer that term). Figure 2-1 provides a diagram of a DOM.

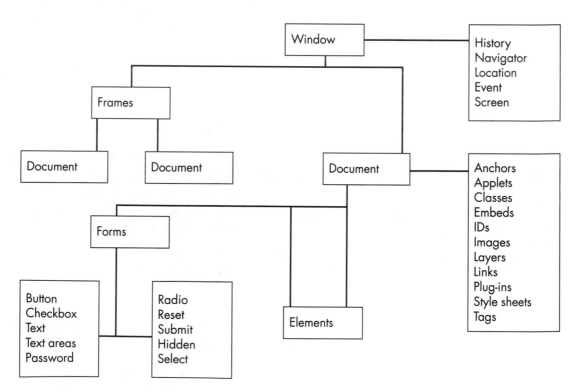

FIGURE 2-1. Document object model hierarchy

As you can see, *Window* is the top-level object, but all elements are attached to the *Document*. The *Window* object is merely the object that contains the *Document*. You do not need to memorize the entire hierarchy. The hierarchy is merely a way of calling objects on the page. If a script needs to refer to an image's style, it might use the following syntax:

window.document.image.style

The actual DOMs for Netscape and Internet Explorer include slight differences in the syntax for calling an object. This variation is one reason for the incompatibility between the two browsers. To refer to the same style in Netscape, we would write this:

document.image.style

To refer to it in Internet Explorer 4.0, we would write this:

document.all.image.style

The image's name would be its ID name. You would specify a style afterward, such as the image's color or position.

In reality, much of the incompatibility of Netscape 4 and Internet Explorer 4 arises from Microsoft's choice of using "all" after "document" in the DOM hierarchy.

NETSCAPE 4.0'S DOM

Netscape has consistently increased the number of objects on the screen that can be controlled using JavaScript. In fact, nearly all HTML and CSS style elements can now be controlled directly via scripting languages. These elements can be described by scripting before the page is written to screen; once written, however, these properties cannot be modified. In other words, unlike in Internet Explorer 4.0, not all properties can be changed at any time. Once written to the screen, only position, visibility, and clipping can be manipulated on the fly. This restriction is why many people consider Netscape 4 to have a much more limited DOM than Internet Explorer 4 has.

Netscape 5 has adopted a different DOM—one that closely resembles Internet Explorer 4.0's DOM and allows all HTML objects and Cascading Style Sheets (CSS) to be updated even after the page is loaded. This new DOM not only closely resembles Microsoft's DOM, but also the DOM proposed by W3C.

INTERNET EXPLORER 4.0'S DOM

Between the release of Internet Explorer version 3.0 and version 4.0, Microsoft made a big step in its DOM. Version 3.0 didn't allow access to the IMG object; version 4.0, in contrast, allows access to all HTML objects as well as to all style sheet properties. What's different in the Internet Explorer 4.0 DOM is that every HTML element is now programmable. Thus any HTML element on the page can be supported by scripting that can interact with user events and change the page content dynamically. This event model enables a document to react when the user has interacted with the page, such as by clicking the mouse on a particular element, pressing a key, or entering information into a form. Each event can be tied to a script that tells the browser to modify the content instantaneously, without returning to the server for a new file. With this DOM, authors will be able to create interactive web sites with fewer pages. Users will not have to wait for new pages to download from web servers, increasing the speed of their browsing and the performance of the Internet as a whole.

As mentioned earlier in this chapter, Microsoft's DOM already closely resembles the DOM proposed by W3C. The Internet Explorer 4.0 DOM is, in turn, merely an extension of the Netscape 3.0 DOM. For years, Netscape has exposed ever more elements to be manipulated by scripting. Microsoft and W3C have simply taken this trend to its logical conclusion and made all elements available for scripting, even after the page has loaded.

W3C'S DOM

Given the confusion and differences between the two version 4.0 browser DOMs, it is good news that W3C has stepped in to create a platform- and language-neutral program DOM. The W3C DOM will allow programs and scripts to access and update the content, structure, and style of documents in a standard way. One major delay in the introduction of this DOM relates to its development for HTML and XML. Because XML is an emerging standard in itself, the process has necessarily been very thorough and deliberate.

The W3C DOM will be proceeding in three steps or levels:

- Level Zero functionality will be equivalent to the DOM available in Netscape 3 and Internet Explorer 3. At the same time, it will address any "bugs" existing in these DOMs and create a standard on which further levels can be built.
- Level One exposes both HTML and XML elements to be accessed and manipulated. It contains functionality for document navigation and manipulation.
- Level Two will include a style sheet object model; it will also define functionality for manipulating the style sheet information attached to a document. In addition, this level will allow rich queries of the document and define some event model.

Additional levels will specify an interface to the possibly underlying window system, including some ways to prompt the user. Finally, the W3C DOM will include some sort of security model.

SUMMARY

The W3C DOM holds great promise as a method of manipulating the properties of both HTML and XML in the future. Reading through much of the early DOM, CSS, and HTML 4.0 specifications, it becomes obvious that the groups are working together to ensure that these three fundamental underpinnings of Dynamic HTML work cohesively.

A unified DOM will go a long way toward making Dynamic HTML a universal standard for interactive multimedia on the web. Because it is built into the browser and requires no plug-ins, it should be able to easily replace technologies such as Java or Shockwave as the multimedia language of choice.

LINKS

ECMAScript
http://www.ecma.ch/stand/ecma-262.htm

WebReview: The Document Object Model Explained
http://webreview.com/97/11/14/feature/concepts.html

Microsoft 4.0 Document Object Model
http://www.microsoft.com/msdn/sdk/inetsdk/help/dhtml/
     doc_object/doc_object.htm

CASCADING STYLE SHEETS:
A BRIEF INTRODUCTION

Controlling the layout of web pages has traditionally been a difficult process. In the beginning, authors had little or no control over the appearance of their pages. Over time, various methods have been developed to lay out elements (graphics and text) on the page in the way that they were originally designed to do. After the introduction of tables, developers adopted this method to help in the layout of elements on the page. In fact, some developers practically have a PhD in table development!

The desire for perfect layout on the page is largely a result of transferring printed material to the web. Print publishers have become accustomed to the control they have over layout in such desktop publishing programs as Adobe PageMaker and Quark Xpress. Translating these printed materials to the web, however, requires precise control over page elements.

With the arrival of **Cascading Style Sheets (CSS)**, developers have achieved this level of control. In addition to pixel-perfect layout, style sheets give authors the ability to layer their content. By stacking layers, developers can create content that they were unable to produce with older browsers. When combined with Dynamic HTML and its animation capabilities, layering truly comes into its own. **Layering** refers to the ability to lay graphics and text over one another (not the **<LAYER>** tag for Netscape 4 that has been superseded by style sheets).

In addition to positioning and layering, CSS also gives the developer control over all aspects of font and text presentation, including font type, spacing, padding, size, and weight. CSS is a true blessing for anyone who has wrestled with trying to make a page look the same in Internet Explorer and Netscape for both the Macintosh and the PC. So you can turn in your table PhD and learn style sheets!

CASCADING STYLE SHEET SUPPORT IN BROWSERS

CSS is supported only in the latest versions of browsers.

Both Netscape Communicator 4 and Internet Explorer 4 fully support CSS, and CSS is compatible between both browsers. As shocking as it may sound, both browsers are fully compatible—well, almost. As a result, CSS is often called the Neutral Zone for the version 4.0 browsers.

What happens with CSS in older browsers? Some, such as Netscape 2.0 and 3.0, are smart enough to ignore style sheets when they are enclosed in the **<style>** tag. If browsers are unable to support CSS, it is preferred that they ignore this tag.

Some even older browsers, such as Internet Explorer 2 and Netscape 1, will ignore the **<STYLE>** tag as well, but display the information between the tags. This information will then be printed at the top of the screen as a single line—and looks terrible. To work around this problem, the information inside the **<STYLE>** tag should be commented out. The style information is then placed inside the **<!-- -- >** tags, as in the following example:

```
<HTML>
      <TITLE>Hiding Style Sheets in
Older Browsers<TITLE>
      <STYLE type="text/css">
            <!--
```

> **TIP**
> ·······
> The first browser to give significant support to CSS was Internet Explorer 3. The web links at the end of the chapter give more information on CSS in this browser.

```
                    #element {
                    POSITION: absolute;
                    Z-INDEX: 1;
                    LEFT: 30px;
                    TOP: 30px;}
                    -->
              </STYLE>
              <BODY>
<div id=element>
<IMG SRC="gallery/element.gif" WIDTH=120
HEIGHT=90 BORDER=0>
</div>

              </BODY>
</HTML>
```

By using this technique, you can ensure that your style sheets gracefully degrade in older browsers.

Differences Between Internet Explorer 4 and Netscape 4

One large difference exists in CSS for Microsoft's and Netscape's version 4 browsers: the visibility attribute. This attribute controls whether the object is initially visible on the screen or remains hidden. It is an especially powerful tool when combined with the DOM and JavaScript. As we will use visibility extensively later in this book, it is a good idea to introduce these differences now. Using JavaScript or VBScript, you can then cause objects to become visible or hidden based on user interaction.

Internet Explorer 4 follows the final W3C reference for this parameter. A visible object has the value "visible." A hidden object is "hidden." In the example we've been using, the graphic element.gif would be visible when this page loads. If the visibility parameter was set to "hidden," then it would still load into memory, but remain hidden from view. The visibility parameter in Listing 3-1 keeps the object visible.

LISTING 3-1. CODE THAT KEEPS AN OBJECT VISIBLE IN INTERNET EXPLORER 4

```
<HTML>
        <TITLE>Hiding Style Sheets in Older Browsers<TITLE>
        <STYLE type="text/css">
                <!--
                #element {
                POSITION: absolute;
                Z-INDEX: 1;
                LEFT: 30px;
                TOP: 30px;
                Visibility:visible}
                -->
        </STYLE>
        <BODY>
<div id=element>
<IMG SRC="gallery/element.gif" WIDTH=120 HEIGHT=90 BORDER=0>
</div>

        </BODY>
</HTML>
```

Netscape brought out its browser just as the final versions of
CSS standards were being ratified. The company guessed at what
the visibility parameters would be—but it guessed wrong. In
Netscape 4, to make an object visible you use "show"; to make it
hidden you use "hide." Listing 3-2 is the same as Listing 3-1, but
includes this change.

LISTING 3-2. CODE THAT KEEPS AN OBJECT VISIBLE IN NETSCAPE 4

```
<HTML>
        <TITLE>Hiding Style Sheets in Older Browsers<TITLE>
        <STYLE type="text/css">
                <!--
                #element {
                POSITION: absolute;
```

```
            Z-INDEX: 1;
            LEFT: 30px;
            TOP: 30px;
            Visibility:show}
            -->
        </STYLE>
        <BODY>
<div id=element>
<IMG SRC="gallery/element.gif" WIDTH=120 HEIGHT=90 BORDER=0>
</div>

        </BODY>
</HTML>
```

Netscape has stated that it will comply with the W3C standard in Netscape 5. It will continue to support "show" and "hide" so as to accommodate older code.

Cursors in Internet Explorer 4

The proprietary CSS property cursor allows the developer to change the cursor shape by making a CSS declaration or by setting the **style.cursor** property dynamically. Table 3-1 lists the possible values for this property.

Default Settings

If the visibility parameter is left out of the style sheet, then by default the object should be shown. Netscape browsers will interpret the object visibility parameter as "show"; Internet Explorer 4 will interpret it as "visible." By eliminating the visibility parameter, you can bypass this incompatibility. Only when you hide and show objects with scripting will you run into the incompatibility.

DIV AND SPAN TAGS

DIV (division) and **SPAN** (to span over an area) are new elements to HTML. These tags were introduced to support style sheets.

TABLE 3-1. CURSORS FOR INTERNET EXPLORER 4

Shape	CSS declaration	script assignment	TEST
↖	cursor: default;	element.style.cursor = "default";	
↔	cursor: move;	element.style.cursor = "move";	
☝	cursor: hand;	element.style.cursor = "hand";	
✛	cursor: crosshair;	element.style.cursor = "crosshair";	
⌛	cursor: wait;	element.style.cursor = "wait";	
☋	cursor: help;	element.style.cursor = "help";	
←	cursor: w-resize;	element.style.cursor = "w-resize";	
↑	cursor: n-resize;	element.style.cursor = "n-resize";	
→	cursor: e-resize;	element.style.cursor = "e-resize";	
↓	cursor: s-resize;	element.style.cursor = "s-resize";	
↖	cursor: nw-resize;	element.style.cursor = "nw-resize";	
↗	cursor: ne-resize;	element.style.cursor = "ne-resize";	
↘	cursor: se-resize;	element.style.cursor = "se-resize";	
↙	cursor: sw-resize;	element.style.cursor = "sw-resize";	
UA	cursor: auto;	element.style.cursor = "auto";	

DIV, the most powerful tag, allows you to create areas on the page. An area is a section of the page with a certain height and width—sort of a floating layer. This area can be treated independently from the rest of the page. For example, it can be animated or hidden, or it can be made transparent or have the graphics within it switched. **DIV** areas can have their own style sheets attached; the style sheets might define the elements within the **DIV** and position them on the page with x, y, and z coordinates. **DIV** is the tag that is commonly used to create an element on the page that will be manipulated independently of the rest of the

> **TIP**
> ......
> **SPAN** can be used only on text that does not include line breaks.

TIP
·······
Do you hate the gray box that appears on the screen while a Java applet loads? You can keep the Java applet hidden until it has finished loading and then make it visible again after it has fully loaded.

page. Such tags can contain several graphics or any combination of elements. They can even provide Java and plug-ins such as Shockwave.

The **SPAN** tag is used to apply a certain type of style sheet to an area of text or graphics without any line breaks. **DIV** tags, on the other hand, can include a line break. Imagine you have a section of text where every third word has the following attributes: bold, Times font, point size 35, underlined, and italic. You're probably saying, "Jeff, I'd never produce something so tacky." But do you remember the time you experimented with the **<blink>** tag? You never know what you'll be asked to produce. Using the **SPAN** tag, you can create all the attributes we discussed earlier and then apply them whenever necessary by calling them. Listing 3-3 gives an example.

LISTING 3-3. USING THE **SPAN** TAG

```
<HTML>
      <Title>Tacky Words</title>
      <Style><!--
            span.tacky {
                  Font-family:times;
                  Font-style: Italic;
                  Font-weight: Bold;
                  Line-height: 35pt;
                  Text-Decoration: underline
                  }-->
      </style>
<body>

Every third <span class=tacky>word</span> in this <span
    class=tacky>sentence</span> is required <span class=tacky>to
    </span> to be tacky.

</body>
</html>
```

DIFFERENCES BETWEEN LAYERS AND STYLE SHEETS

I'm not convinced that there is any reason to learn the **<LAYER>** tag for Netscape 4. This tag was a "cludge" that was invented before style sheets were implemented. It was presented to the W3C standards body as part of the standards for CSS1 and was turned down.

In Netscape 4, both layers and the **DIV** tag are supported as ways of designating parts of a page. Imagine that you wanted to animate a part of the page. You could designate that part with either a **DIV** or **LAYER** tag and then animate it. The **LAYER** tag is supported only in Netscape 4, however, while the **DIV** tag is supported in both Netscape 4 and Internet Explorer 4. The **LAYER** tag will probably continue to be supported in future releases of Netscape, but it will never be cross-platform-compatible. In fact, Netscape now indicates that it will fully support CSS as the method of choice for creating sections of the page. In the end layers, the **DIV** tag provides identical functionality without the incompatibility of the **LAYER** tag. Netscape has recently clarified its position regarding the **LAYER** tag:

> *Myth 3: Netscape's Dynamic HTML is based on the LAYER tag.*
>
> Netscape fully supports the use of the syntax specified in the W3C working draft "Positioning HTML Elements Through Cascading Style Sheets" (http://www.w3.org/TR/WD-positioning), coauthored by engineers at Netscape and Microsoft and supported by Netscape Communicator 4.0, to achieve the functionality available through the LAYER tag. (Source: http://search.netscape.com/communicator/comparison/realstory.html)

LINKING DIV TAGS AND STYLE SHEETS

In Listings 3-1 and 3-2, we linked the style sheet to the element it will position. We titled the style sheet "element." The "element" style sheet was then used to position the graphic element.gif. (It is not necessary to give the style sheet and the graphic the same name.) We then used **<div id="element">** to link the positioning information with the graphic.

PLACEMENT OF STYLE SHEETS

Style sheets can be placed at two places on a page. I prefer the method shown in Listing 3-4, where the style sheet remains separate from the elements of the page.

LISTING 3-4. KEEPING THE STYLE SHEET SEPARATE FROM THE ELEMENTS OF THE PAGE

```
<HTML>
      <TITLE>Hiding Style Sheets in Older Browsers<TITLE>
      <STYLE type="text/css">
            <!--
            #element {
            POSITION: absolute;
            Z-INDEX: 1;
            LEFT: 30px;
            TOP: 30px;
            }
            -->
      </STYLE>
      <BODY>
<div id=element>
<IMG SRC="gallery/element.gif: WIDTH=120 HEIGHT=90 BORDER=0>
</div>
      </BODY>
</HTML>
```

An alternative method is to include the style sheet in-line with the element, as in the following example:

```
<IMG SRC="gallery/element.gif" WIDTH=120
HEIGHT=90 BORDER=0
style="position:absolute; left:30;
top:30; z-index:1">
```

The graphic element.gif will display 30 pixels from the left side of the screen and 30 pixels from the top and in layer 1. The positioning applies to the upper-left corner of the graphic.

This method of placing the style information in-line with the element it defines has both advantages and disadvantages. On the plus side, it retains the information about the element and its positioning in the same place. On the minus side, it doesn't allow a central repository for all style information, unlike the **<STYLE>** tag. It also doesn't allow the style information to be reused by other elements on the page.

POSITIONING OF ELEMENTS ON THE SCREEN

The most important function of style sheets is their placement of elements on the screen. The first parameter, **POSITION**, defines what the element is positioned relative to. In "Absolute" positioning, the element is placed relative to the upper-left corner of the screen, which is the 0,0 coordinate. In "relative" positioning, the element is positioned relative to another element. This method is rarely used, however, and we will not show it here.

The **LEFT** and **TOP** parameters are the x and y coordinates of the upper-left corner of the element being positioned. In other words, if you want to position a graphic so that its upper-left corner is 30 pixels from the top of the browser window and 30 pixels over from the left margin, you would use the style sheet in Listing 3-4.

The **Z-INDEX** parameter allows elements to be placed on top of one another or layered. The higher the number, the closer the element appears to the viewer. If layer 1 included a graphic and layer 2 included text, and the two overlapped, then the text would rest on top of the graphic. This property allows an author to create composite images from several screen elements.

FONT DEFINITIONS

CSS gives you total control over the presentation of fonts. Table 3-2 lists some of the most important tags for controlling the appearance of fonts. All of these attributes can be placed into the style sheet, just as the other attributes were included in earlier examples. The order doesn't matter, and you aren't required to use them all.

TABLE 3-2. FONT TAGS

`Font-family: Times;`	Font family name
`Font-style: Normal;`	**Normal** is the default, but **Italic** and **Oblique** are also available
`Font-variant: Normal;`	**Normal** and **Small-caps**
`Font-weight: Bold;`	**Bold** and **Normal**, or 100–900, with 100 being the lightest
`Font-Size: 12px;`	Expressed in point size (pt) or pixels (px)
`Line-height: 14pt`	Also called **Leading**, it is the distance between lines of text
`Text-transform: uppercase`	**Capitalize**, **uppercase**, **lowercase**, or **none**
`Text-Decoration: underline`	**underline**, **overline**, **line-through**, and **blink**

T I P

Using pixel size to define fonts helps to make the fonts have the same size when they appear in different browsers and on different operating systems.

SPACING

Spacing attributes are similar to the attributes of cellspacing and cellpadding in tables. If you envision a **DIV** area as a single cell in a table, then you might want to give this area a border and a margin and perhaps define its height and width. Figure 3-1 diagrams how spacing attributes are defined.

The list of properties that you can specify to define these areas is nearly endless. We will not delve into them all, but rather seek a basic understanding of them.

MARGINS, PADDING, AND BORDERS

You can refer to Table 3-3 when you're thinking about how to implement these parameters. I rarely use margins, padding, or borders. If an object should be 5 pixels away from another object, I don't set the margin to 5 pixels. Instead, I change the **TOP** and

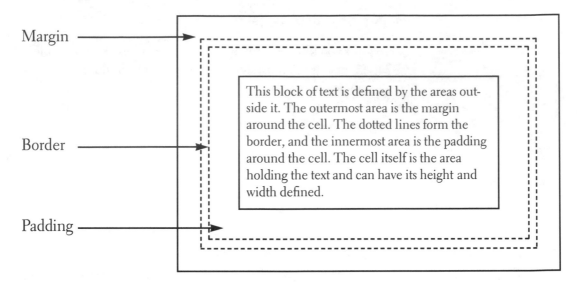

Margin

Border

Padding

This block of text is defined by the areas outside it. The outermost area is the margin around the cell. The dotted lines form the border, and the innermost area is the padding around the cell. The cell itself is the area holding the text and can have its height and width defined.

FIGURE 3-1. Spacing attributes

LEFT properties so that its *x* and *y* positions are altered by 5 pixels. In general, I use these properties in conjunction with the background-color parameter to create colored blocks behind text. Using margins, you can create a colored border behind the text without using a GIF image as a color block.

TABLE 3-3. MARGIN, PADDING, AND BORDER TAGS

`Margin:5pt;`	Sets all margins (top, bottom, left, and right) to 5 points. You may also use a percentage of the width of the **DIV** area.
`Margin-top;`	Margin at the top of the **DIV** area
`Margin-bottom;`	Margin at the bottom of the **DIV** area
`Margin-left;`	Margin at the left of the **DIV** area
`Margin-right;`	Margin at the right of the **DIV** area
`Padding:5pt;`	Sets all padding (top, bottom, left, and right) to 5 points. You may also use a percentage of the width of the **DIV** area.
`Padding-top;`	Padding at the top of the **DIV** area
`Padding-bottom;`	Padding at the bottom of the **DIV** area
`Padding-left;`	Padding at the left of the **DIV** area

continued

TABLE 3-3. MARGIN, PADDING, AND BORDER TAGS *(Continued)*

`Border:5pt;`	Sets all borders (top, bottom, left, and right) to 5 points. You may also use a percentage of the width of the **DIV** area.
`Border-top;`	Border at the top of the **DIV** area
`Border-bottom;`	Border at the bottom of the **DIV** area
`Border-left;`	Border at the left of the **DIV** area
`Border-color:blue;`	Sets the color of the border area
`Border-style:dashed;`	Sets the style of lines: **none** (default), **dotted**, **dashed**, **solid**, **double**, **groove**, **ridge**, **inset**, **outset**

> **TIP**
>
> The auto function does not always work correctly.

WIDTH AND HEIGHT

The width and height define the **DIV** area. If these properties are not defined, an auto function will calculate how much room is needed to display the information in the **DIV** tag. Table 3-4 shows the tags used for these attributes.

Imagine that a **DIV** area contains an image that is 200 pixels wide. When the user places the mouse over this **DIV** area, the image should change. Sometimes the **DIV** area will extend well beyond the 200 pixels that should enclose the image. It is always a good idea to include the width of the **DIV** area as a parameter.

TABLE 3-4. WIDTH AND HEIGHT TAGS

`Width:240px;`	The width of the **DIV** area is 240 pixels
`Height:320px;`	The height of the **DIV** area is 320 pixels

TEXT ALIGNMENT

You may need to left-justify text within the **DIV** tag. This tag, shown in Table 3-5, allows you to justify any element, graphics, text, or Java applet within the **DIV** area.

TABLE 3-5. TEXT ALIGNMENT TAG

`Text-align:center;`	Parameters: **center**, **left**, **right**

BACKGROUND COLOR AND IMAGE

You may wish to set the background color of the **DIV** area. This color will then show behind whatever else appears in the **DIV** block. If the **DIV** area contains text, then the text will have a colored background; if the area holds a transparent GIF image, then the background color will show around it.

You may also include a background image for the **DIV** area. This type of tiled image serves the same function as the body background for the entire web page.

Table 3-6 lists tags to control background color and image.

TABLE 3-6. BACKGROUND COLOR AND IMAGE TAGS

`Background-color:#996633;`	Allows you to make the entire **DIV** background a certain color. Useful for colored blocks behind text or images.
`Background-image:url(dot.gif)`	The default is **none**. Remember to put "url" in front of the path name.

Many more tags are available for CSS1 besides those described here. Most of them do relatively obscure things with text that I have chosen not to cover. Entire books have been written on the subjects covered so briefly in this chapter. For reliable if somewhat technical information on style sheets, try the specifications published by W3C (http://www.w3c.com). Alternatively, you might purchase a book such as *Cascading Style Sheets: Designing for the Web* by Hakon Wium Lie and Bert Bos.

THE FUTURE: CSS2

As of the writing of this book, only a working draft of Cascading Style Sheets 2 (CSS2) had been published. Some differences between CSS1 and CSS2 were apparent in this document.

Media Type

Web pages contain data that may be presented in several different ways. For example, the data may be printed out, read on screen, or projected onto a wall. Eventually, the information may be interpreted and turned into Braille for the blind or read aloud in your car. To prepare for this eventuality, the Media Type parameter was created so that web pages could communicate with the devices that are reading them. I can't wait to have the headlines read to me in my car from washingtonpost.com.

Paged Media

This parameter will give you greater control over the physical size of the page. It is actually an extension of the box model used for padding, borders, and margins. It allows page breaks, and lets you control how the material is presented based on which page you are on. This property may eventually be useful for contextual navigation. For example, if you're on the last page, then you may be able to present the navigation bar without using the Next Page button.

Aural Media

The spoken word comes to the web with these style sheets for having the page read aloud. The proposed controls will manage volume, pausing, mixing of sounds, and cueing of sounds before playing. This parameter also allows you to choose different styles of voices for reading the page. This option may be hooked into a plug-in for the browser or into the text-to-speech function of the operating system.

Other attributes that are proposed for CSS2 include automatic numbering of pages and better font embedding and downloading.

CSS2 appears poised to allow web pages to better communicate with other media types. It will also give the developer greater control over page elements.

SUMMARY

CSS represents another step in breaking down the web creation process into manageable parts. By separating the layout and content, we can reuse style sheets multiple times to present similar information. This flexibility not only saves time during download-ing, but also allows for a central repository where one change can update many pages.

Although CSS1 has gone a long way toward giving web developers a formal layout language, it will be extended in the future to help lay out other media types besides graphics and text. With CSS2, it is already being extended to handle sound. In Internet Explorer 5, it is used to help attach standard behaviors to HTML objects. Keeping these behaviors external means that the objects can be reused many times. When XML enters the picture, CSS will provide the framework into which all media are poured.

LINKS

Cascading Style Sheets in Internet Explorer 3
http://www.microsoft.com/mind/1096/cascading/cascading.htm

Style Sheet Compatibility Chart
http://www.webreview.com/guides/style/mastergrid.html

Cascading Style Sheets in Internet Explorer 4
http://www.microsoft.com/workshop/author/css/css-ie4-f.htm

Cascading Style Sheets in Netscape 4
http://developer.netscape.com:80/viewsource/angus_css.html

W3C Cascading Style Sheets 1 Standards
http://www.w3.org/TR/REC-CSS1

CSS2
http://www.w3.org/TR/REC-CSS2/

MOUSEOVERS

Scripting can be difficult, but useful examples can make it much easier to learn such new skills. If you can take an example and apply its lessons soon after studying it, then you will gain the confidence to take the example apart. After you understand one example, then you can extend those skills to other, similar scripts. Nothing is more useful or easier to perform than the mouseover scripts in Netscape 4 and Internet Explorer 4.

Mouseovers are extremely popular with users. A **mouseover** takes place when an object changes as the mouse pointer moves over it. It may consist of a graphic change or a change in text color. Most users know that a **rollover** indicates that the area is clickable. One problem with the web is that every web site presents a different interface. Many authors assume that they know how people will react while surfing. Most users actually react based on intuition and instinct. They click on whatever looks interesting; they don't take the time to understand that a particular interface is based on the geometric patterns inherent in pre-Babylonian architecture. People are especially attracted to animation, and mouseovers provide the animation for which they are looking. Images that change during a mouseover attract the eye and demand to be clicked on.

Because mouseover scripts are generally compatible with a variety of browsers, they are relatively easy to show and to plug right into your web pages. Note that this is the only chapter where the examples will work in version 3 browsers. All other examples in this book will be pure Dynamic HTML.

BROWSER COMPATIBILITY WITH MOUSEOVER SCRIPTS

JavaScript has come a long way in the last couple of years. Only recently, however, has it given you access to the image object. In other words, only recently has JavaScript allowed you to swap images. Table 4-1 explains which browsers support imaging swapping.

TABLE 4-1. BROWSER SUPPORT OF IMAGE SWAPPING

Browser	Image Swap Support
Netscape 1	No JavaScript support
Netscape 2	No; some JavaScript support, but no image swap support
Netscape 3	Yes
Internet Explorer 2	No
Internet Explorer 3 (PC)	No
Internet Explorer 3 (Macintosh)	Yes; the Macintosh version, which came out later than the PC version, supported image replacement
Internet Explorer 4	Yes

TEXT ROLLOVERS

Users generally know that they should click on underlined words to follow a link. In addition to underlining words, you can change the color, size, or font of a word when you move the mouse over it. Figure 4-1 gives an example of a mouseover color change.

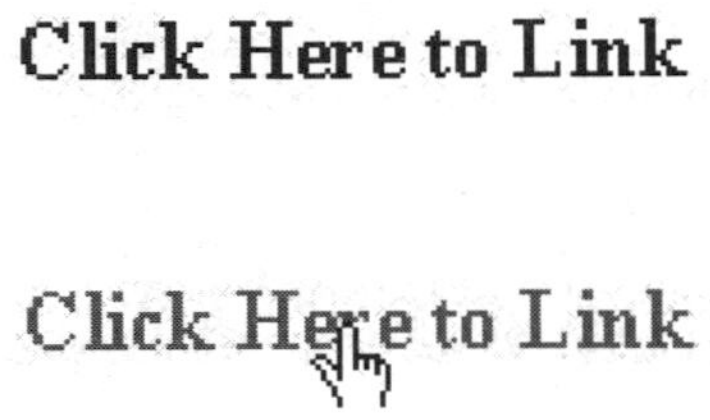

FIGURE 4-1.
Text color change on
mouseover

Click Here to Link

Click Here to Link

You can also add extra text, so that only a keyword shows until mouseover occurs; a whole sentence then pops up. This swapping of text can significantly enhance the user's experience while adding very little to the total download time. Remember the first rule of web development, however: Text is cheap, but graphics are expensive.

The new text rollovers work only in Netscape 4 and Internet Explorer 4. Although older browsers supported the image object, they did not provide a way to swap text. If you want to swap text in an older browser, you must create graphics of the text and perform the swapping with graphics. This approach makes it harder to change your text, but it's the only way to do so.

Internet Explorer 4's DOM exposes the style sheet information for text, making it very easy to change text when the mouse moves over it. With one very simple JavaScript command, you can change the color of the text, for example. Listing 4-1 gives the script for this command.

LISTING 4-1. INTERNET EXPLORER 4 SCRIPT FOR A TEXT COLOR CHANGE ON MOUSEOVER

```
<HTML>
<HEAD>
    <TITLE>IE4 Mouseover Text</TITLE>
</HEAD>

<BODY>
<a href="http://www.ruleweb.com/dhtml/"
onmouseover="javascript:this.style.color='blue'"
```

```
onmouseout="javascript:this.style.color=""><b>DHTML
    Demos</b></a>

</BODY>
</HTML>
```

Notice that we use a shortcut to tell JavaScript which object needs its color changed. We use "this" to let JavaScript know that we are talking about the text within the **HREF** tag. We change the style to the color **blue**. Now when the mouse is over the text, the text is blue; when the mouse leaves, the text returns to its original color.

Looks easy, doesn't it? You may be less happy when you see what it takes to accomplish the same task in Netscape 4. Because Netscape does not expose all HTML objects to JavaScript, we must fall back on the **document.write** command to perform the dynamic updating. This demo is a bit of a cludge relative to the Internet Explorer 4 script. If you need to write a cross-platform page, however, then this method is the only way to do it. Listing 4-2 provides the relevant script for Netscape 4 (found at http://www.ruleweb.com/dhtml/text/NS4Text.html).

> **TIP**
> ⋯⋯
> The original color can be designated by empty quotation marks (" ") or you can enter the color name.

LISTING 4-2. NETSCAPE 4 SCRIPT FOR A TEXT COLOR CHANGE ON MOUSEOVER

```
<html>
    <TITLE>Netscape 4 Mouseover Text</TITLE>
<head>
<script language="JavaScript1.2">

function changeto(){
setTimeout(changeto1, "1");
}

function changeto1() {
document.layers["text"].document.write("<font color=Blue><a
    href=http://www.discovery.com>Link to Discovery</a></font>");
```

```
document.layers["text"].document.close();
}

function changefrom(){
setTimeout(changefrom1, "1");
}

function changefrom1() {
document.layers["text"].document.write("<font color=red>Link to
    Discovery</font>");
document.layers["text"].document.close();
}

function link() {

}
</script>
</head>

<body bgcolor="Black">
<layer name="text" top=150 left=0 width=200 height=30
    onmouseover=changeto() onmouseout=changefrom()>
<font color="Red">Link to Discovery</font>
</layer>

</body>

</html>
```

Quite a contrast between the Internet Explorer 4 version and the Netscape 4 version, isn't there? If you need to produce a cross-platform version of the mouseover text script, we recommend using a graphic of the text and studying the examples provided later in this chapter. If that option is not acceptable, you can use an **IF THEN** statement so that Netscape 4 sees its own code and Internet Explorer 4 sees separate code. (**IF THEN** statements were covered in Chapter 1.) Even the Netscape code isn't particularly elaborate. It just seems excessive because the same mouseover change is so easy to accomplish in Internet Explorer.

Certain performance issues arise when you use the Netscape script. On slow computers, with many mouseover links present you may see slight delays before the highlighted link appears. This lag reflects the processor-intensive nature of swapping the content of the layer. If you run your mouse down a line of buttons with mouseovers, for example, there will be some delay before the mouseover image appears.

GRAPHIC ROLLOVERS

Text is nice, but a picture is worth a thousand words—at least according to the cliché. Image swapping on mouseovers has been around since Netscape 3 and even Internet Explorer 3 for the Macintosh. The first method we'll explore is a cross-platform method.

There are two ways to swap out images. The original and most cross-platform-compatible method is to swap the image object. This method works in Netscape 3 and 4 as well as Internet Explorer 4 and Internet Explorer 3 for Macintosh. It does not work in Internet Explorer 3 for PC, but it also does not produce any error messages in this browser. Error messages are generated by using object detection. You've previously seen browser detection, which determines the browser that you are using and substitutes the appropriate code. With object detection, only browsers that support the image object will use the mouseover code. Thus only browsers capable of doing the mouseover will try to display it. This method is better than browser detection because it will work in Internet Explorer 5 and Netscape 5 without forcing you to rewrite code. With browser detection, you'll have to modify the code when these new browsers are released.

The second method to swap out images is to hide one image and show another when the mouse moves over the image. This method works only in the version 4 browsers, and there is even some incompatibility between them because of the differences in the *visibility* property of style sheets. (Remember "show" versus "visible" from Chapter 3?)

Swapping the Image Object

Listing 4-3 gives the code for swapping an image object. A demonstration of this universal mouseover is located at http://www.ruleweb.com/dhtml/MouseOver/universal.html.

LISTING 4-3. SWAPPING AN IMAGE OBJECT

```
 1. <HTML>
 2. <HEAD>
 3. <TITLE>Universal Image Rollovers</TITLE>

 4. <SCRIPT LANGUAGE="JavaScript">
 5. <!--
 6. if (document.images) {    //If image object is available
 7. img1on = new Image();       // Mouseover images
 8. img1on.src = "image1on.gif";
 9. img2on = new Image();
10. img2on.src = "image2on.gif";
11. img3on = new Image();
12. img3on.src = "image3on.gif";
13. img4on = new Image();
14. img4on.src = "image4on.gif";

15. img1off = new Image();          // Mouseout images
16. img1off.src = "image1off.gif";
17. img2off = new Image();
18. img2off.src = "image2off.gif";
19. img3off = new Image();
20. img3off.src = "image3off.gif";
21. img4off = new Image();
22. img4off.src = "image4off.gif";
23. }
```

```
24. function imgOn(imgName) {
25. if (document.images) {
26. document[imgName].src = eval(imgName + "on.src");          }}

27. function imgOff(imgName) {
28. if (document.images) {
29. document[imgName].src = eval(imgName + "off.src");         }}

30. //-->
31. </SCRIPT>
32. </HEAD>
33. <BODY BGCOLOR = "#FFFFFF">

34. <A HREF = "http://www.ruleweb.com" onMouseOver =
    "imgOn('img1')" onMouseOut = "imgOff('img1')">
35. <IMG NAME= "img1" BORDER = 0 HEIGHT = 65 WIDTH = 65 SRC =
    "image1off.gif"></A>

36. <A HREF = "http://www.ruleweb.com/dhtml/" onMouseOver =
    "imgOn('img2')" onMouseOut = "imgOff('img2')">
37. <IMG NAME= "img2" BORDER = 0 HEIGHT = 65 WIDTH = 65 SRC =
    "image2off.gif"></A>

38. <A HREF = "http://www.ruleweb.com/dhtml/html/whatsnew.html"
    onMouseOver = "imgOn('img3')" onMouseOut = "imgOff('img3')">
39. <IMG NAME= "img3" BORDER = 0 HEIGHT = 65 WIDTH = 65 SRC =
    "image3off.gif"></A>

40. <A HREF = "http://www.ruleweb.com/dhtml/html/reviews.html"
    onMouseOver = "imgOn('img4')" onMouseOut = "imgOff('img4')">
41. <IMG NAME= "img4" BORDER = 0 HEIGHT = 65 WIDTH = 65 SRC =
    "image4off.gif"></A>

42. </BODY>
43. </HTML>
```

After taking a quick look at the script, you should see that this universal mouseover isn't too difficult to understand. Let's look at it line by line.

Lines 6–23:

```
 6. if (document.images) {        //If image object is available
 7. img1on = new Image();        // Mouseover images
 8. img1on.src = "image1on.gif";
 9. img2on = new Image();
10. img2on.src = "image2on.gif";
11. img3on = new Image();
12. img3on.src = "image3on.gif";
13. img4on = new Image();
14. img4on.src = "image4on.gif";

15. img1off = new Image();        // Mouseout images
16. img1off.src = "image1off.gif";
17. img2off = new Image();
18. img2off.src = "image2off.gif";
19. img3off = new Image();
20. img3off.src = "image3off.gif";
21. img4off = new Image();
22. img4off.src = "image4off.gif";
23. }
```

Line 6 is the statement that detects whether the browser is capable of using the image object. If the browser can use the image object, then it can perform mouseovers.

Lines 7–22 load the images into memory so that when the mouseovers occur the over graphics are already downloaded. These lines also set the real image name, such as **image1on.gif**, to a variable, such as **img1on.src**. This step allows us to use one function for the on and off states. Reusing the same function for all graphics enables us to write a more compact script with less download time. If you wanted to add more graphics than the four shown, you would simply add more lines and increase the numbers by one. For example, imagine that you want to add a fifth graphic. Just include the following lines:

Add after Line 14:

```
img5on = new Image();
img5on.src = "image5on.gif";
```

Add after Line 22:

```
img5off = new Image();
img5off.src = "image4off.gif";
```

Add in the Body of HTML:

```
<A HREF = "http://www.ruleweb.com/dhtml/html/reviews.html"
    onMouseOver = "imgOn('img5')"onMouseOut = "imgOff('img5')">
<IMG NAME= "img5" BORDER = 0 HEIGHT = 65 WIDTH = 65 SRC =
    "image5off.gif"></A>
```

As you can see, we simply changed the numbers to "5" and added another image. We continued to use the same functions, **imgOn** and **imgOff**.

Lines 24–29:

```
24. function imgOn(imgName) {
25. if (document.images) {
26. document[imgName].src = eval(imgName + "on.src");    }}

27. function imgOff(imgName) {
28. if (document.images) {
29. document[imgName].src = eval(imgName + "off.src");    }}
```

These two functions are the heart of the rollovers. Let's look at **imgOn** first. If the user rolls over the first image,

```
<A HREF = "http://www.ruleweb.com"
onMouseOver = "imgOn('img1')" onMouseOut
= "imgOff('img1')">
<IMG NAME= "img1" BORDER = 0 HEIGHT = 65
WIDTH = 65 SRC = "image1off.gif"></A>
```

then the variable **img1** is passed to the function. This variable, **imgName**, is substituted into the function. Thus the source (**src**) is changed for the image. Instead of displaying **img1off.src**, the browser now displays **img1on.src**. As you may remember, **imgon.src** is actually the image **image1on.gif**. All that is happening is a rash of substituting that allows us to use one function for all mouseovers.

The second function is even simpler. When the mouse moves off the graphic, then the function simply replaces the original image.

Lines 34–41:

```
34. <A HREF = "http://www.ruleweb.com" onMouseOver =
    "imgOn('img1')" onMouseOut = "imgOff('img1')">
35. <IMG NAME= "img1" BORDER = 0 HEIGHT = 65 WIDTH = 65 SRC =
    "image1off.gif"></A>

36. <A HREF = "http://www.ruleweb.com/dhtml/" onMouseOver =
    "imgOn('img2')" onMouseOut = "imgOff('img2')">
37. <IMG NAME= "img2" BORDER = 0 HEIGHT = 65 WIDTH = 65 SRC =
    "image2off.gif"></A>

38. <A HREF = "http://www.ruleweb.com/dhtml/html/whatsnew.html"
    onMouseOver = "imgOn('img3')" onMouseOut = "imgOff('img3')">
39. <IMG NAME= "img3" BORDER = 0 HEIGHT = 65 WIDTH = 65 SRC =
    "image3off.gif"></A>

40. <A HREF = "http://www.ruleweb.com/dhtml/html/reviews.html"
    onMouseOver = "imgOn('img4')" onMouseOut = "imgOff('img4')">
41. <IMG NAME= "img4" BORDER = 0 HEIGHT = 65 WIDTH = 65 SRC =
    "image4off.gif"></A>
```

These lines of HTML display the initial graphics on the page. Notice that each graphic is named with an **IMG NAME**. These names tell the script which graphic needs to be swapped during a mouseover. Also notice the **onMouseOver** and

onMouseOut events. In line 34 in the **onMouseOver** event, the **imgOn** function is triggered and the variable **img1** is passed to the function.

If you stick with the naming conventions set up here, then you can develop as many mouseovers as you wish.

Multiple Images Displayed on Rollover

Having one image change on mouseover is fine, but what if you want to roll over a button and have another graphic pop up in another part of the screen as well as having the button accomplish a rollover? We can build on Listing 4-3 to accomplish just that. In fact, with only a few minor changes, we can have a second graphic pop up. In Listing 4-4, the new code appears in bold italics. (An example of this code is located at http://www.ruleweb.com/dhtml/MouseOver/multiuniversal.html.)

LISTING 4-4. POPPING UP A SECOND GRAPHIC WHILE SWAPPING AN IMAGE OBJECT

```
 1. <HTML>
 2. <HEAD>
 3. <TITLE>Universal Image Rollovers</TITLE>

 4. <SCRIPT LANGUAGE = "JavaScript">
 5. <!--
 6. if (document.images) {        //If image object is available
 7. img1on = new Image();         // Mouseover images
 8. img1on.src = "image1on.gif";
 9. img2on = new Image();
10. img2on.src = "image2on.gif";
11. img3on = new Image();
12. img3on.src = "image3on.gif";
13. img4on = new Image();
14. img4on.src = "image4on.gif";

15. img1off = new Image();        // Mouseout images
16. img1off.src = "image1off.gif";
```

```
17.  img2off = new Image();
18.  img2off.src = "image2off.gif";
19.  img3off = new Image();
20.  img3off.src = "image3off.gif";
21.  img4off = new Image();
22.  img4off.src = "image4off.gif";

23.  img1ad = new Image();
24.  img1ad.src = "image1tips.gif";   // Secondary Images
25.  img2ad = new Image();
26.  img2ad.src = "image2tips.gif";
27.  img3ad = new Image();
28.  img3ad.src = "image3tips.gif";
29.  img4ad = new Image();
30.  img4ad.src = "image4tips.gif";
31.  }

32.  function imgOn(imgName) {          if (document.images) {
33.  document[imgName].src = eval(imgName + "on.src");
34.  document["holder"].src = eval(imgName + "ad.src");
35.  }}

36.  function imgOff(imgName) {          if (document.images) {
37.  document[imgName].src = eval(imgName + "off.src");
38.  document["holder"].src = "clear.gif";          }}

39.  //-->
40.  </SCRIPT>
41.  </HEAD>
42.  <BODY BGCOLOR = "#FFFFFF">
43.  <A HREF = "http://www.ruleweb.com" onMouseOver =
     "imgOn('img1')" onMouseOut = "imgOff('img1')">
44.  <IMG NAME= "img1" BORDER = 0 HEIGHT = 65 WIDTH = 65 SRC =
     "image1off.gif"></A>

45.  <A HREF = "http://www.ruleweb.com/dhtml/" onMouseOver =
     "imgOn('img2')" onMouseOut = "imgOff('img2')">
```

```
46.  <IMG NAME= "img2" BORDER = 0 HEIGHT = 65 WIDTH = 65 SRC =
     "image2off.gif"></A>

47.  <A HREF = "http://www.ruleweb.com/dhtml/html/whatsnew.html"
     onMouseOver = "imgOn('img3')" onMouseOut = "imgOff('img3')">
48.  <IMG NAME= "img3" BORDER = 0 HEIGHT = 65 WIDTH = 65 SRC =
     "image3off.gif"></A>

49.  <A HREF = "http://www.ruleweb.com/dhtml/html/reviews.html"
     onMouseOver = "imgOn('img4')" onMouseOut = "imgOff('img4')">
50.  <IMG NAME= "img4" BORDER = 0 HEIGHT = 65 WIDTH = 65 SRC =
     "image4off.gif"></A>

51.  <p>

52.  <!-- Description graphic -->
53.  <IMG NAME = "holder" HEIGHT = 40 WIDTH  = 250 SRC =
     "clear.gif">
54.  </BODY>
55.  </HTML>
```

Figure 4-2 shows the results produced by Listing 4-4.

Notice how few lines of code we needed to add to make another graphic pop up. In lines 23–30, we added code that describes the additional images that should pop up when the mouseover happens. We also assigned variable names to these graphics.

In line 34, we added a line to the **ImgOn** function so that it would swap a new image into the **holder** image.

In line 38, we made sure that when the mouseout event occurs, the original graphic is replaced. In this case, the original graphic is called **clear.gif**.

In line 53, we created a graphic called **holder** that initially displays a blank graphic (a transparent graphic best used as the initial placeholder). When the user moves the mouse over the other graphics, the source for this graphic changes to other graphics with descriptions of the buttons being explored by the user.

FIGURE 4-2.
Mouseovers created by
Listing 4-4

This is the partners area where you can contact our partners

SUMMARY

Many other methods can be used to perform image swapping in the version 4.0 browsers. Images can be hidden and shown by using the visibility parameter of style sheets. In Netscape, layers can be used to show and hide images so as to change the visibility of different layers. While many image swapping methods are available in Dynamic HTML, the best ones are those that support the most browsers. The examples given in this chapter will work in some of the version 3.0 browsers as well as the version 4.0 ones. If you use image object detection instead of browser detection, these scripts should work well in the version 5.0 and later browsers. Remember, a great script is one you never have to touch again after you write it.

LINKS

Web Coder Demo
http://www.webcoder.com/howto/article.html?number=6,
     length=4,demo=1,source=1

Webreference
http://www.webreference.com/js/column1/

TRANSITIONS AND FILTERS

TRANSITIONS IN INTERNET EXPLORER 4

One thing that differentiates web pages from television is the poor use of transitions. Television images seamlessly fade from one to the next through a series of wipes and fades. In contrast, web pages have discordant jumps and flashes of color, often revealing a new page that is only partially loaded. This poor transitioning is the mark of an immature medium—one that still needs to have its rough edges smoothed.

Transitions are really filters applied over time. Their role is to visually move a page or graphic from one state to the next. Many filters can be applied dynamically to create wipes and fades. In addition, certain filters are not transitions, such as drop shadows and glows. These filters produce effects similar to those in Adobe Photoshop. After seeing these filters in action, you will probably agree that they are very crude renderings. Graphics designers are unlikely to put aside Eye Candy and KPT filters in favor of these options in the near future.

A number of early attempts were made to create transitions between pages. One of the first uses of JavaScript was to fade the background to black before transitioning to the next page. Such crude methods represented an attempt to make the user experience images that were less jarring and more pleasing to the eye. Television has had 40 years to smooth out its rough edges; the web has only had a few years to achieve the same feat. Attempts to improve the web user's experience are ongoing.

Transitions can be used at two different times, either inside a page or when switching between pages. As we discussed in Chapter 1, the move from page- to stage-based presentation on the web makes both methods important. Fortunately, transitions are among the easiest multimedia effects to apply.

Underlying Technology

As with many Dynamic HTML effects we will encounter in the course of development, the transition effects for Internet Explorer 4 and Netscape 4 are incompatible. Unlike some other functions, which can be made compatible through clever scripting, we must resort to **IF THEN** statements to create cross-platform effects. (**IF THEN** statements are covered in Chapter 1.)

Microsoft has taken a far more sophisticated approach to transitions. It has built special commands into the Cascading Style Sheets (CSS) that allow authors to produce both transitions and filters without scripting. (For more information on CSS, see Chapter 3.)

Between-Page Transitions (Interpage Transitions)

Interpage filters, illustrated in Figure 5-1, are used between pages, much like the transitions in a slideshow presentation. Microsoft has provided 24 separate effects (listed in Table 5-1) for between-page transitions, all of which are very easy to implement. The **META** tag specifies the type of transition, duration, and other variables, as well as whether the transition should occur as the following page is loaded or as it is exited. The code, which appears in Listing 5-1, should be placed in the **<HEAD>** tag.

These transitions are triggered by an event. In Listing 5-1, the event is the loading and unloading of a page. We will discuss other events that can trigger transitions later in this chapter.

> **TIP**
>
> Internet Explorer 4's filters won't be replacing Adobe Photoshop anytime in the near future.

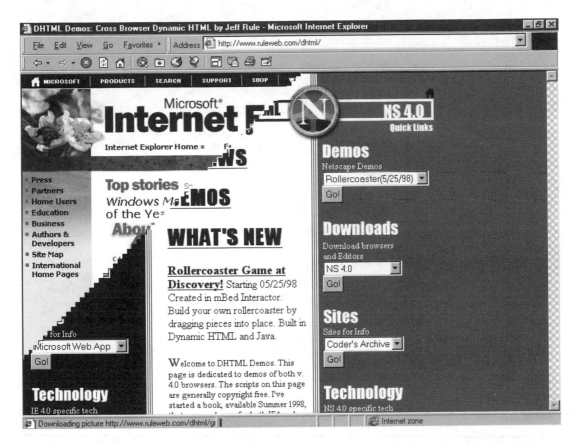

FIGURE 5-1. Transitions in Internet Explorer 4

LISTING 5-1. CODE FOR BETWEEN-PAGE TRANSITIONS

```
<META http-equiv="Page-Enter"
CONTENT="RevealTrans(Duration=4,Transition=1)>
<META http-equiv="Page-Exit"
CONTENT="RevealTrans(Duration=2.500,
    Transition=6)>
```

Variables

By making a few simple changes to the statements in List-ing 5-1, the web developer can create 24 different effects when entering or leaving a page.

TABLE 5-1. INTERNET EXPLORER 4 TRANSITION NAMES AND NUMBERS

Transition Name	Number	Transition Name	Number
Box In	0	Random Dissolve	12
Box Out	1	Split Vertical In	13
Circle In	2	Split Vertical Out	14
Circle Out	3	Split Horizontal In	15
Wipe Up	4	Split Horizontal Out	16
Wipe Down	5	Strips Left Down	17
Wipe Right	6	Strips Left Up	18
Wipe Left	7	Strips Right Down	19
Vertical Blinds	8	Strips Right Up	20
Horizontal Blinds	9	Random Bar Horizontal	21
Checkerboard Across	10	Random Bar Vertical	22
Checkerboard Down	11	Random	23

Page-Enter: This variable controls the transition as the page loads and the way the content is revealed.

Duration: This variable controls the time (in seconds) that the transition should endure. For the **Page-Enter** example in Listing 5-1, the time period is 4 seconds.

Transition: This variable specifies the transition to be used. The transition in Listing 5-1 is set for 1, which is the Box Out transition.

Page-Exit: This variable controls the way that the content is wiped from the screen before the next page is loaded. It makes use of the same variables as **Page-Enter**.

Same-Page Transitions (Intrapage Transitions)

Transitions can also be applied to elements on a page. Pictures can fade into each other, one element can be wiped clear, and another image can be loaded in the background. It is important to remember that with stage-based web development, clearing the page no longer means having to load another page. Transitions that occur on the same page are treated much like filters, and they are applied through style sheets. (See Chapter 3 for more information on style sheet layout.)

Images can be transitioned in two ways:

filter:blendTrans: This filter type fades the image in view. It has only one parameter, Duration. The Fade filter allows the user to control how long it takes the image to fade into view or fade away.

filter:revealTrans: This filter type allows the user to use the 24 transition types. A Wipe filter, it uses two parameters, Duration and Transition.

These transitions are applied by making a function call triggered by an event such as an onload, onclick, or mouseover.

In Listing 5-2, the Fade filter is used to cause the image.jpg graphic to fade up over a period of 2.5 seconds.

LISTING 5-2. USE OF A FADE FILTER

```
<HTML>
<HEAD>
<TITLE>Intrapage Transitions</TITLE>

<SCRIPT LANGUAGE="VBSCRIPT">
<!--
Sub Window_onload()
      Call pic 1_show()
End Sub

Sub pic1_show()
      pic1.filters(0).apply()
      pic1.style.visibility = "visible"
      pic1.filters(0).play()
End Sub
```

```
-->
</SCRIPT>
<BODY>
<IMG id="pic1" SRC="image.jpg" WIDTH=300
    HEIGHT=408 BORDER="0" style="position:
    absolute; left: 100; top: 100; z-index: 1;
    visibility: hidden; filter:blendTrans
    (duration=2.50)">
</BODY>
</HTML>
```

To cause the image to fade out again, you would use an event to trigger another function to hide the image. Here's an example:

```
Sub pic1_hide()
      pic1.filters(0).apply()
      pic1.style.visibility = "hidden"
      pic1.filters(0).play()
End Sub
```

Once again, the image will fade out over a period of 2.5 seconds.

The ability to fade images in and out will reach its full usefulness when combined with a sequencing script. We will discuss timeline scripts in Chapter 10.

The Wipe filter is applied in much the same way. Simply insert the following code into the filter parameter:

```
filter: revealTrans(Transition=4,
Duration=1.5)
```

Other Resources

Many other examples of transitions are available on the web. Try the following sites for more demos and examples:

Jason and Garth's Demos: Walk through all of the Internet Explorer 4 transitions at http://drg.microsoft.com/dhtml/demos/transition/transall.htm

Microsoft samples: http://www.microsoft.com/msdn/sdk/inetsdk/help/dhtml/content/filters.htm#CSS_Filters

Fading graphics: http://www.ruleweb.com/dhtml/Transitions/trans2.html

FILTERS IN INTERNET EXPLORER 4

Filters, whose use is illustrated in Figure 5-2, are effects that can be applied to certain HTML objects. The objects to which they are most typically applied are text and graphics, but they can also be applied to a wide range of other objects. Table 5-2 provides a full list.

The current incarnation of filters is rather crude. The filters have a grainy, nonprofessional look, particularly the Glow and Drop Shadow filters. For the near future, I would recommend applying these filters to images and text in Photoshop or some other image editor. Table 5-3 lists the filters available for Internet Explorer 4.

Some other filters can prove very useful. The Opacity filter, when applied over time, allows the user to fade images in and out. The FlipH and FlipV filters allow an author to reverse the direction of an image when the image's animation reverses direction. Use these filters sparingly, and they can greatly reduce your download times for images and minimize your use of animated GIF images.

Some filters—such as Shadow, Drop Shadow, Glow, and Mask—require transparency to function properly. Text automatically has "transparency," or space around the characters that shows through to the object (or page) behind it. GIF images must be in gif89a format with a transparent color to display these filters properly.

This isn't my Photoshop's Blur Filter

The Drop Shadow Filter

Glow needs work

Vertical Flip Filter

The Wave Filter in Action

Mask Filter

FIGURE 5-2. Filters in Internet Explorer 4

TABLE 5-2. OBJECTS TO WHICH FILTERS CAN BE APPLIED

BUTTON	
DIV	(with a defined height, width, or absolute positioning)
IMG	
INPUT	
MARQUEE	
SPAN	(with a defined height, width, or absolute positioning)
TABLE	
TD	
TEXTAREA	
TFOOT	
TH	
THEAD	
TR	

Source: http://www.microsoft.com/msdn/sdk/inetsdk/help/dhtml/content/
filters.htm.

Underlying Technology

The filters use Microsoft's proprietary technology
degrade well, however, as we discussed in Chapte
place a drop shadow on a word and then present the page in
Netscape, no errors will occur and the word will appear normally
but without the drop shadow. This useful feature allows the filters
to be used to enhance Internet Explorer users' experience without
making the page unviewable in Netscape.

The main problem with certain graphic filters, such as Drop
Shadow and Glow, is that they are applied to text with aliased
edges.

Performance Issues

Filters must be calculated in real time when they are applied. As a
result, there are performance issues associated with the use of filters. The user's machine must be fast enough to calculate these
filters while the page is loading. It is not recommended that filters
be viewed on machines below a 133-Mhz Pentium. Filters may
take a few seconds to render once they are displayed, and this lag
must be taken into account by the developer. It is also useless to
try to change the look of a filter dynamically before it renders
the first time. The effects that make the greatest performance
demands are the lighting effects, drop shadows, and transparency.

A variety of methods are employed to create filters' effects.
Transparency filters, which control opacity effects, act on each
pixel individually. Glow filters, on the other hand, inherit their
effects from the pixels around them, creating a fading sensation
toward the edge of the effect.

Filter Application

Filters can be applied in two ways: statically or dynamically. **Static filters** are unchanging. An example would be applying a drop
shadow to text. **Dynamic filters** are applied over time. An example would be to have the glow filter pulse around some text.

TABLE 5-3. INTERNET EXPLORER 4 FILTERS

Filter Effect	Parameters	Description
Alpha	Opacity 1–100	Sets a transparency level
Blur	Direction 0–360 Strength Length of pixel blur	Creates the impression of moving at high speed
Chroma	Color = #RRGGBB	Makes a specific color transparent
Drop Shadow	OffX=#of pixels OffY=#of pixels Color=Color of drop shadow	Creates an offset solid silhouette
FlipH	None	Creates a horizontal mirror image
FlipV	None	Creates a vertical mirror image
Glow	Color Strength 1–255	Adds radiance around the outside edges of the object
Grayscale	None	Drops color information from the image
Invert	None	Reverses the hue, saturation, and brightness values
Light		Projects light sources onto an object
Mask		Creates a transparent mask from an object
Shadow		Creates a solid silhouette of the object
Wave		Creates a sine-wave distortion along the x-axis and y-axis
X-Ray		Shows just the edges of the object

Source: Based on data from http://www.microsoft.com/msdn/sdk/inetsdk/help/
dhtml/content/filters/Visual_Filter.htm#Visual_Filter.

Static Filters

As we mentioned earlier (see Table 5-2), filters can be applied to many HTML objects. Typically they are applied to text or graphics. In Listing 5-3, we apply a drop shadow to an image. The red shadow is offset 5 pixels along the x- and y-axes.

LISTING 5-3. APPLICATION OF A STATIC FILTER (DROP SHADOW)

```
<HTML>
<HEAD>
<TITLE>Drop Shadow Filter</TITLE>
</HEAD>
<BODY>
<img id=image1
    src=" http://www.ruleweb.com/dhtml/drag/ie_gear.jpg ">
<p>
<img id=image2
    src=" http://www.ruleweb.com/dhtml/drag/ie_gear.jpg " style=
    "filter:DropShadow(color=red, OffX=5, OffY=5)">

</BODY>
</HTML>
```

Dynamic Filters

As noted earlier, the filter set that accompanies Internet Explorer 4 is primitive at best. You should use the dynamic filters especially sparingly in design work. They are not meant to replace the plug-ins that accompany Photoshop or other graphics programs. If used to make words pulse or flip back and forth in horizontal orientation, they can be even more annoying than the old **<BLINK>** tag.

Because dynamic filters take place over time, they are usually accompanied by a timeline script (discussed in detail in Chapter 10). In Listing 5-4, the script causes text to gradually apply and unapply various filters. (Ignore the time intervals in this script for now.)

LISTING 5-4. APPLICATION OF DYNAMIC FILTERS

```
<HTML>
<HEAD><TITLE>Dynamic Filter Demos</TITLE>
<SCRIPT>
function init()
{
```

```
        makeFlash(txt1)
        setInterval("txt2.filters.alpha.opacity =
    (txt2.filters.alpha.opacity + 5) % 101", 100)
        setInterval("foo(txt3)", 100)
}
var delta = 5
function foo(obj)
{
        if ((obj.filters.alpha.opacity + delta > 100)
        || (obj.filters.alpha.opacity + delta < 0))
                delta = -delta
        obj.filters.alpha.opacity += delta
}
function makeFlash(obj)
{
        obj.flashTimer = setInterval("txt1.filters.glow.enabled =
    !txt1.filters.glow.enabled", 1000)
}

</SCRIPT>

</HEAD>
<BODY onload="init()">
<DIV id=txt1 style="width:50%;
    filter:glow(Color=#FAF900,Strength=2,enabled=0);"><H1>Glow
    Effect</H1></DIV>
<DIV id=txt2 style="width:50%; filter:alpha(opacity=100);"><H1>Fade
    Effect</H1></DIV>
<DIV id=txt3 style="width:50%; filter:alpha(opacity=50); color:
    blue"><H1>Fade Up and Down</H1></DIV>
</BODY>
</HTML>
```

TRANSITIONS IN NETSCAPE

Netscape Communicator does not contain any built-in transition
or filter effects in the same way that Internet Explorer 4 does. In

fact, the Netscape browser makes no provisions for interpage transitions or filters at all. Some intrapage effects can be applied by JavaScript functions to images, but these scripts are considerably more complicated than the ones used in Internet Explorer 4. The limited number of Netscape interpage transitions we will discuss here use the "clipping" technique for layers. As we discussed in Chapter 3, **LAYER** is a tag that will not be used in the Dynamic HTML DOM being developed by W3C. Netscape may support it in later versions, but it will never be a cross-browser solution.

Underlying Technology

Most transition effects created for Netscape use the clipping effect for layers. By changing how a layer is clipped, we can give the appearance of a transition. Clipping controls how much of the layer is currently visible. It is similar to the cropping function provided in Photoshop. If clipping increases from showing very little of the layer to showing the whole layer, then the layer appears in a wipe. By making the clipped regions invisible and gradually incrementing these regions, we can create the effect of wiping both the layer and the image it contains. Chapter 3 gives more information on layers.

Horizontal Wipe

The horizontal wipe gives the effect of a barn door closing. It works by reducing the right and left clipping widths by 6 pixels after each increment, as shown in Listing 5-5. The IF statement at the end of the code determines when the effect ends. To prevent any clipping that results in negative numbers, all negative numbers are automatically set to zero, thereby preventing any over-clipping of the layer.

A horizontal wipe is only one variation on this transition. Other directional variations can be used as well.

LISTING 5-5. HORIZONTAL WIPE

```
<html>
<head>
```

```
<title>Example of Sliding Layers</title>

<script language="JavaScript">

function curtainWidth(lyr,xinc,inctime,stopwidth)  {
lyr.clip.left += -(xinc/2)
lyr.clip.right += (xinc/2)
if (lyr.clip.width < 0) {lyr.clip.width = 0}
if (((xinc < 0) && (lyr.clip.width > stopwidth))  ||
    ((xinc > 0) && (lyr.clip.width < stopwidth)))  {

setTimeout('curtainWidth(document.layers["'+lyr.name+'"], '+xinc+',
    '+inctime+', '+stopwidth+')',inctime)

}
}

</script>

</head>
<body bgcolor="#ffffff"
onload="curtainWidth(document.layers['vsbar'],-6,15,0)">
<layer name="vsbar" top=100 left=100 visibility=inherit
    clipwidth=500 width=500>
<img
src="http://developer.netscape.com/news/viewsource/images/bnr_sub_
    viewsource.jpg"
width=490 height=32 alt="View Source Title Bar">
</layer>

</body>
</html>
```

Let's look at the parameters that you can modify in List-ing 5-5. The parameters are stored in the onload command. The current values are **['vsbar'],-6,15,0)**.

`lyr.name`: The layer's name in this example is **vsbar**.

`xinc`: This variable tells the function how many pixels to make invisible with each repetition of the function. With each repetition, 6 pixels are clipped from the right and left side of the layer. This process repeats itself until the entire image is clipped.

`inctime`: This parameter controls how often the clipping function is repeated. In Listing 5-5, it happens every 15 milliseconds (1,500 milliseconds = 1.5 seconds). The faster the function is repeated, the smoother the animation will look. A balance must be struck, however, between smoothness and taxing the machine's redrawing capabilities. Many machines will have problems redrawing the image every 15 milliseconds.

`stopwidth`: This parameter tells the function to stop repeating when the clipping area reaches a certain width. In this case, it stops at 0 when the layer has completely disappeared.

Several other parameters must be changed if you wish to insert an image with a different height and width. The only number that matters in this case is the width, as the wipe occurs horizontally. The layer width must be modified to match the width of the graphic or the graphic wipe will occur off-center. In Listing 5-5, the width is 500. The layer width differs from the clip width, which does not need to be changed.

Other Wipe Variations

Several other wipes can be prepared based on this basic theme of clipping the layer.

Vertical Wipes

To build a function to handle vertical versions of the wipe in Listing 5-5, we simply replace the width, left, and right references with names denoting height, top, and bottom. This new function is called **curtainHigh**.

Spotlight Sweep

By modifying a layer's clipping rectangle, we can produce the effect of a spotlight sweeping across the image, revealing the image only where the spotlight shines. This effect is created by incrementing a small clipping rectangle so that it passes across the image. The following parameters are used:

lyr: The name of the layer to which the effect is applied.

litewidth: The width of the revealed spotlight area in pixels.

inctime: The time it takes the image to increment once (in milliseconds).

lyrwidth: The width of the layer; same as width of the image.

xstep: The number of pixels that the spotlight increments each time. Small increments produce smoother animations, but they hurt performance.

direction: The direction in which the spotlight travels; it is positive for right-to-left movement and negative for left-to-right movement.

SUMMARY

Netscape and Microsoft have chosen to implement transitions and filters in very different ways. Microsoft has provided a large number of built-in effects that allow us to do wipes and fades between pages as well as similar transitions for HTML elements on the page. These effects, however, are proprietary to Internet Explorer 4. In addition to not being compatible with Netscape browsers, these PC-based transitions and filters are also not compatible with Internet Explorer 4.0 for Macintosh and UNIX. While Microsoft has promised that these effects will be added to the Macintosh platform eventually, this vow makes little difference now. For most developers, once a browser is released, it must be supported. At Discovery Channel, for example, we make an effort to support all browsers. If users with Internet Explorer 4 for Macintosh and users with Internet Explorer 4 for Windows are to view the same page, then we won't be able to use these transitions.

Another issue to consider relates to performance. Wipes and fades between pages appear crude and jerky on any machine less powerful than a 266-MHz Pentium II. Transitions and filters that happen within a page are more reliable, but still should be tested on the slowest machine that your users might own.

The filters that accompany Internet Explorer 4 are also crude in comparison with the effects available in Adobe Photoshop. In particular, the Drop Shadow and Glow filters appear pixelated and grainy. Other filters, such as the Opacity (alpha) filter, are much more useful. Use these filters sparingly, and they can provide a nice addition to your web development arsenal.

Netscape has not provided any built-in transition or filter effects. Transitions must be created via more complicated JavaScript coding. I have provided several examples of wipes and transitions that you can implement on your own pages. These transitions take advantage of the clipping feature of Netscape's **LAYER** tag and are completely different from any Internet Explorer 4 implementation.

Creating a cross-browser solution for transitions can be difficult. The web developer must make use of both **IF THEN** techniques and browser detection to succeed in providing compatibility.

> **TIP**
> ·······
> Transitions look good only on high-end machines.

LINKS

Netscape Transitions

http://developer.netscape.com/news/viewsource/
    angus_layers.html
http://www.webreference.com/dhtml/column13/

RESIZING GRAPHICS

BACKGROUND

Dynamic HTML promises increased functionality without increased download time, but it does not always live up to its promise. Sometimes developers go wild with these new effects and start recreating CD-ROM interfaces on the web. This excess can dramatically increase download time. Even the author has been guilty of this sin. After trying to show some of my bloated work over a 28.8 modem, however, I was quickly cured by being acutely embarrassed when it took two minutes for one page to load. After the initial period of excitement over Dynamic HTML's possibilities wears off, good developers start to think how adding a few lines of code can make for a better interface. Remember: adding code to your page is cheap, but adding new graphics or video is very expensive.

At Discovery, I often work with media assets that were developed for older browsers, generally static graphics with the occasional animated GIF thrown in. I always ask how these assets can be extended into Internet Explorer or Netscape Communicator and used to better tell a story. If a picture is worth a thousand words, then a moving dynamic picture must be worth at least a million. By taking a static image and either moving it or causing it to change shape and size, I can improve the user interface without increasing download time! Chapter 9 will cover animations, but for now let's talk about how resizing graphics can add to the user experience.

RESIZING OPTIONS

People are attracted to motion; it is hard-wired into our brains. That's one reason why you'll spend two hours viewing a movie, but won't spend two minutes looking at a web page. Motion draws attention to important parts of the web page. It highlights areas and conveys the information that the area is important.

Currently on the web, several methods are used to draw attention to a clickable area. Text that represents a hyperlink is underlined. Another (now extinct) method was to have the text `<BLINK>`. Designers all over the world rejoiced when the `<BLINK>` tag went out of fashion. Graphics attract attention by changing on rollover, which usually requires another graphic downloading for the mouseover state. Another increase in bandwidth is then necessary, especially if the entire menu bar includes rollover graphics.

Bulge

One method of attracting attention is to have the graphic "bulge" when the user mouses over the graphic. This option offers a simple and effective way to attract attention without downloading a mouseover graphic. In a bulge, the graphic scales through a number of steps to approximately 120% of its original size and then collapses back to normal. This rise and collapse is done by triggering a short script that causes the graphic to resize. If many graphics of the same size make up the navigation bar, for example, you can use a single short script to give them all a rollover effect.

Growing a Graphic to Fill the Screen

Imagine, if you will, a series of small, thumbnail pictures of the left side of the screen that are arranged vertically. When the user runs the mouse over each picture, it resizes to become four times its original size and text appears underneath it. This option is a great way to convey lots of information in a relatively limited space—one of the strengths of the version 4.0 browsers. For example, in a Web interface developed by Corbis, four graphics that all touch one another are arranged in a box shape. When the user clicks on one graphic, the picture expands to fill the entire box and cover the other pictures temporarily. After a few seconds, it collapses back to the original size.

Show and Collapse

We used the show-and-collapse technique at Discovery in our Zoo story for Internet Explorer 4. You can see it at http://www. discovery.com/area/nature/zoo/tour1.1.html (Figure 6-1).

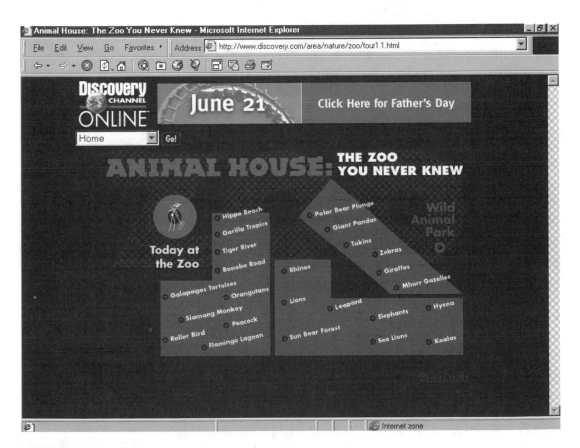

FIGURE 6-1. Zoo Interactive

Using this method, a number of large pictures can be presented on the screen. After a few seconds, they will resize down to thumbnail-size pictures. Many large pictures can be presented this way and then scaled down and made into a navigation bar. This process can be repeated for many pictures. By using a time-based presentation method, the author can present one aspect of the site and then clear it away and show another picture. On Discovery's Zoo site, the collapsing graphic also went through several graphic "swaps" as it collapsed. In other words, we substituted several graphics while resizing them, to produce a "morphing" effect from the larger graphic to a button. The resulting story presented an interface that was simply impossible with older browsers, but was still relatively low bandwidth.

Disappear

Making a graphic disappear from the screen can be difficult to accomplish. Internet Explorer contains a number of transitions and wipes that make this operation easier. It is much more difficult to create transitions for Netscape browsers. (See Chapter 5 for further details on transitions.)

Resizing the graphic can be a good transition. For example, having one graphic collapse to zero height and width, and then substituting another graphic that expands back to full size, can be used as a transition between graphical presentations.

Moving While Resizing

In January 1998, we worked on a story about the B2 Stealth Bomber at Discovery. The story included a flying sequence in which the B2 Bomber races across the whole screen, avoiding radar and finally dropping its bomb on a factory (Figure 6-2). The perspective taken was from the top down. What we would have liked to do, but which deadlines prohibited us from trying at the time, was to show the screen from another perspective—one in which the plane streaked into the screen, giving the screen a sense of depth. Ideally, the image of the bomber would have started off large and gradually shrunk as it crossed the screen and then dropped its bomb. It would have continued to recede until it

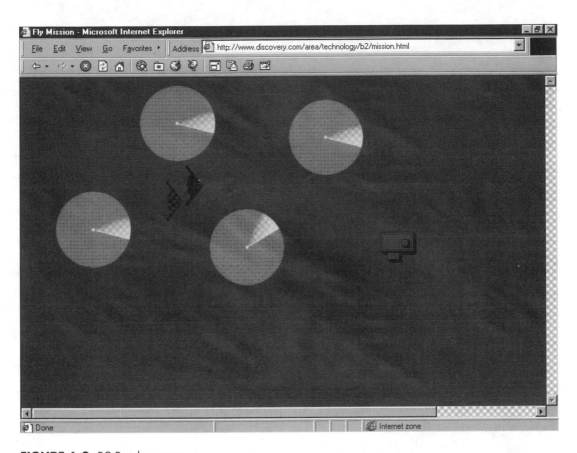

FIGURE 6-2. B2 Bomber game

"disappeared in the distance" with its size at zero height and width. We could never get this image to work properly, because taking the image from very large to very small didn't work very well with GIF images. Perhaps you could coax this operation into working in one of your stories, however, so don't be afraid to give it a shot.

> **T I P**
> ·······
> Remember that scaling an image too much can make it look pixelated.

TECHNICAL ISSUES

Image resizing is a very new feature in the 4.0 browsers. Because of this, little compatibility exists between browsers. As you will find, what is easy to do in Internet Explorer 4 is difficult or impossible to do in Netscape 4.

Browser Issues

The examples in this chapter are mainly for Internet Explorer 4. Unfortunately, this browser has more elements "exposed" to JavaScript than Netscape 4. One element that is not exposed, however, is the width and height of images. Thus a graphic can not have its width and height dynamically changed once it is written to the screen. To perform resizing in Netscape, the image must be placed in a layer or **DIV**. Layers are then rapidly swapped to give the impression of a growing image, with each layer presenting an image that is slightly larger. As you can imagine, this method is very resource-intensive and the transition is less than smooth. With the release of Netscape 5, all of these elements should be exposed and a truly cross-platform image resizing script should be possible.

The examples for Netscape 4 given in this chapter use a different method. By replacing graphics in a layer with the **document.write** command, the author can give the impression of dynamic updating. Unfortunately, this method results in a jerky transition from one graphic to the next. The same effect could be accomplished by showing and hiding a number of layers or **DIV** areas in rapid succession.

Performance Issues

Resizing graphics in real time is a challenge for your CPU, unless you're running a high-end machine. Although I normally do my development on a high-end machine, I test the Dynamic HTML playback on low-end machines as well. If graphic resizing occurs in one step (for example, going from a thumbnail at 30×40 to a large image at 300×400), then the computer can handle this operation along with several other tasks. On the other hand, if you scale the image so that a smooth transition between sizes occurs, then much more of the computer's capacity is used.

To circumvent this problem of capacity, it is a good idea to have no more than three animations happening at any one time.

Imagine that you have a graphic animation across the top of the screen. You should make sure that two other graphics aren't resizing at the same time. The result of too many simultaneous animations can be jerky performance, stalling, and even scripting errors.

Practical Resizing

Two types of graphics exist: vector graphics and raster graphics. The two are not created equally when it comes to resizing.

Vector graphics are line art like that produced in programs such as Adobe Illustrator and Macromedia Freehand. When these graphics are scaled up or down, they do so smoothly without producing artifacts. They are not in wide use on the web. In fact, Internet Explorer 4.0 is the only browser that supports them without a plug-in or Active X control.

Raster graphics are used most often on the web. Typical raster graphics are JPEG and GIF files. These images generally don't scale well. Scaling of these images looks best between about 80% and 120% of the original size. Above or below these sizes, the image develops "artifacts" that consist of blurring, patches of color, and loss of detail. For quick animated mouseovers, this development is not a problem. When an image is blown up to 200% of its original size, however, it develops these artifacts. GIF and JPEG images generally scale down better than they scale up. Thus it may be a good idea to bring in a large image at a small size, and then scale it up to its true size. Another solution is to hide a small thumbnail image and then replace it with the image you intend to scale just as the scaling begins.

UNDERLYING TECHNOLOGY

The examples for resizing graphics in this chapter are all written in JavaScript. Most of these scripts use a few simple techniques. The graphics are increased in size by using a **FOR ELSE** loop. With this loop, the width (or height) of the graphic is increased by 5-pixel increments until it reaches a certain size, then something else occurs. Usually, the "something else" is an end to the growth or a hesitation before the graphic shrinks back to its original size.

By using these simple loops, you can create a number of great special effects for your web pages.

EXAMPLES

In the following examples, we'll provide the code needed to perform a variety of resizing tasks.

Basic Resizing (Internet Explorer 4)

In this example, the graphic makes the jump between a small thumbnail and a large graphic in one step. While this effect may not have as much "wow" factor as a graphic that smoothly resizes between a small and large size, it is functional and doesn't tax the processor as much. It is also an effect that was impossible to achieve with older browsers. You may have occasionally seen graphics resize on older browsers, but this change was accomplished with a huge animated GIF file. Using this technique is not only easier than creating an animated GIF, but also much more bandwidth-effective.

Bulge (Internet Explorer 4)

As we discussed earlier, having a graphic briefly bulge in size when the mouse rolls over it is an effective method of attracting attention. It lets the user know that the area is clickable or has some important meaning.

The bulge script, as shown in Listing 6-1, is relatively simple. Translated into English, it says the following: The original graphic is 99 pixels wide by 128 pixels high. When the mouse rolls over the graphic, it triggers the **expand** function. This function increases both the height and the width by 5 pixels. It keeps increasing the size by 5-pixel increments until the width equals 110 pixels. At this point, it triggers the **reduce** function, which says that if the width is greater than 99 pixels, then reduce the graphic's size in increments of 5 pixels until the width is again 99 pixels.

LISTING 6-1. BULGE EXAMPLE

```
1.  <!DOCTYPE HTML PUBLIC "-//W3C//DTD HTML 3.2//EN">
2.  <HTML>
3.  <HEAD>
4.  <!--START meta tags-->
5.  <META NAME="description" CONTENT="Discovery Online">
6.  <META NAME="keywords" CONTENT="">
7.  <!--END meta tags-->
8.  <TITLE>Discovery Online</TITLE>
9.
10.     <script language="JavaScript1.2">
11.
12.     function expand() {
13.           if (smallslot.width<=110) {
14.                 x=window.setTimeout('expand()', 10)
15.                 smallslot.width=smallslot.width + 5
16.                 smallslot.height=smallslot.height + 5
17.           }
18.           else {
19.                 setTimeout('reduce()', 0)
20.     }
21.           }
22.
23.     function reduce() {
24.           if (smallslot.width>99) {
25.                 x=window.setTimeout('reduce()', 10)
26.                 smallslot.width=smallslot.width - 5
27.                 smallslot.height=smallslot.height - 5
28.           }
29.     }
30.     </script>
31.
32.     <body bgcolor="White" text="Black">
33.
34.     <div id="slot1" style="width:99;height:128"
    onmouseover=expand()>
```

```
35.      <a href="http://www.discovery.com" target="_top">
36.      <IMG id="smallslot" SRC="980116denali.gif" WIDTH=99
    HEIGHT=128 hspace=0 vspace=0 border=0 style="position:absolute;
    left:296; top:104;z index:2;visibility:visible"></a>
37.      </div>
38.
39.      </body>
40.      </html>
```

Listing 6-1 is nice and short—just the way we like a script to be. To tear it apart line by line, we will work backward through the code, starting with the graphic (we need the graphic before we can start doing things to it).

Lines 34–37:

```
34. <div id="slot1" style="width:99;height:128"
    onmouseover=expand()>
35. <a href="http://www.discovery.com" target="_top">
36. <IMG id="smallslot" SRC="980116denali.gif" WIDTH=99 HEIGHT=128
    hspace=0 vspace=0 border=0 style="position:absolute; left:296;
    top:104;z index:2;visibility:visible"></a>
37. </div>
```

In this chunk of code we are creating a **<div>** area called **slot1** that is 99 by 128, the same size as the graphic. Inside the **<div>** tag is the graphic **smallslot**, which is also 99 by 128. We also set the style information, including the location where the graphic appears on the page and the layer that contains it. (See Chapter 3 for more information on style sheets.)

Once the **slot1 <div>** area has the mouse run over it, we'll trigger the **expand** function.

Lines 12–21:

```
12. function expand()  {
13. if (smallslot.width<=110)  {
```

```
14. x=window.setTimeout ('expand()', 10)
15. smallslot.width=smallslot.width + 5
16. smallslot.height=smallslot.height + 5
17. }
18. else {
19. setTimeout ('reduce()', 0)
20. }
21. }
```

The **expand** function operates as follows: It checks the **smallslot1** graphic. If the graphic's width is less than or equal to 110 pixels, the function increases the width by 5 pixels. It sets up a loop to check and resize this image until the size equals 110 pixels. The loop in line 14 continues to call the same function, looping after waiting 10 milliseconds. This small hesitation between loops allows the graphic to redraw on the screen and gives the appearance of a smooth expansion. If the time here were set to zero, then the graphic would appear to jump between width 99 and width 110.

Once the graphic reaches 110 pixels wide, then the **else** section of the function (line 18) begins. It triggers the **reduce** function after waiting zero milliseconds. If you wanted the graphic to grow and then wait a second before shrinking, you would increase this time from zero to some number. Remember that time is measured in milliseconds (1,000 milliseconds = 1 second).

The **reduce** function is shown in lines 23–29.

Lines 23–29:

```
23. function reduce()  {
24. if (smallslot.width>99)  {
25. x=window.setTimeout ('reduce()', 10)
26. smallslot.width=smallslot.width - 5
27. smallslot.height=smallslot.height - 5
28. }
29. }
```

This function checks to see whether **smallslot**'s width is greater than 99. As the graphic has been expanded to 110 pixels, the function reduces the size by 5 pixels and continues to loop until the size equals 99 pixels—where the graphic initially began. Once this operation is complete, the graphic is ready to be triggered again when the mouse rolls over it.

Move While Resizing (Internet Explorer 4)

Having a graphic move while resizing lets the graphic appear to move in all three dimensions at once. It can move vertically or horizontally, and to a limited extent it can resize to give the impression that it's moving toward the viewer. In fact, someone is undoubtedly putting on red-and-blue 3-D glasses and trying to create the first 3-D web page. You also may want to combine some of the resizing scripts shown in Listing 6-2 with the animation scripts that are discussed later in this book (Chapter 9).

LISTING 6-2. MOVE WHILE RESIZING EXAMPLE

```
1.  <HTML>
2.  <HEAD>
3.  <script language="JavaScript1.2">
4.  var m=0;

5.  function scale() {
6.     m++; //increase by 1
7.     if ( m<=30) {
8.        x=window.setTimeout ('scale()', 100); //calls itself
9.        scaleGraphic(10);
10.            moveGraphic(5);
11.     }
12.  }

13.    function moveGraphic (moveIncrement) {
14.        graphic.style.pixelLeft = graphic.style.pixelLeft +
    moveIncrement;
15.    }
```

```
16.     function scaleGraphic(scaleIncrement) {
17.           graphic.width = graphic.width + scaleIncrement;
18.     }

19.     </script>

20.     </HEAD>
21.     <BODY BGCOLOR="#FFFFFF" TEXT="#000000" onload=scale()>
22.

23.     <IMG id=graphic style="position:absolute;left:0;top:0;"
   width=0 SRC="http://www.ruleweb.com/dhtml/Resize/interfac.jpg">

24.     </BODY>
25.     </HTML>
```

Lines 4–12:

```
4. var m=0;

5. function scale () {
6. m++;
7. if ( m<=30) {

8.    x=window.setTimeout ('scale()', 100);
9. scaleGraphic(10);
10. moveGraphic (5);
11.    }
12.    }
```

The first thing that happens in Listing 6-2 is that the first variable is declared. In this case, we simply set **m** equal to zero. This variable will be used in the **scale** function to indicate how many times the function should be run. When the function starts in line 5, **m** is increased by 1. In JavaScript, **++** means to increase a value by 1. Line 7 then checks whether **m** is less than 30. Since **m** is equal to 1 at this point, it lets the function execute. In line 8, the number 10 is passed to the **scaleGraphic** function and the number 5 is passed to the **moveGraphic** function. These values will be used to tell the graphic how much to increase in size and how much to move for each of the 30 times that the **scale** function executes. In line 10, the function waits 100 milliseconds ($\frac{1}{10}$ second) before executing again. The next time the function is executed, **m** will be equal to 2. This loop will continue until **m** = 30; the function will then stop.

Lines 13–18:

```
13. function moveGraphic(moveIncrement)  {
14.         graphic.style.pixelLeft = graphic.style.pixelLeft +
    moveIncrement;
15. }

16. function scaleGraphic(scaleIncrement)  {
17.         graphic.width = graphic.width + scaleIncrement;
18. }
```

Lines 13–18 are the two functions to which the scale function was passing numbers. The **moveGraphic** function received the number 5. This function takes the graphic's distance from the *y* axis and adds 5 to it. The graphic then moves 5 pixels to the right. When this function is executed 30 times, it will move the graphic 150 pixels to the right.

At the same time, the **scaleGraphic** function increases the width of the graphic by 10 pixels each time. This change causes the graphic to grow gradually, eventually reaching a width of 300 pixels.

Lines 21–23:

```
21. <BODY BGCOLOR="#FFFFFF" TEXT="#000000" onload=scale()>
22.
23. <IMG id=graphic style="position:absolute;left:0;top:0;" width=0
    SRC="http://www.ruleweb.com/dhtml/Resize/interfac.jpg">
```

In line 21, **onload=scale()** causes the **scale** function to start executing as soon as all elements of the page are loaded. This command is essential because we don't want to start animating our graphic until it has been downloaded. Line 23 merely shows the graphic and sets the graphic ID to **graphic**, so that we can reference it in the functions. (Note: You do not need to name the graphic file "graphic"; you can name it anything you want.)

Netscape Resizing

Because Netscape browsers were introduced earlier than Internet Explorer was, they don't have all the functionality of Internet Explorer. Netscape 5 may be able to use the Internet Explorer 4 examples shown previously. In the meantime, there are certain tricks you can use to simulate dynamic graphic resizing in Netscape 4.

In Listing 6-3, we'll create a layer, then swap the same image into this layer using the **document.write** command. Each time we swap in the image, it will be slightly larger. This procedure makes for a jerky change in size, but it's the best we can do.

LISTING 6-3. RESIZING IN NETSCAPE 4

```
1.  <html>
2.  <head>
3.  <script>

4.  function start() {
5.  setTimeout(resize, "2000");
6.  }

7.  function resize() {
8.  document.layers["interface_layer"].document.write("<IMG
    SRC=http://www.ruleweb.com/dhtml/Resize/interfac.jpg width=120
    align=left>");
9.  setTimeout(resize1, "1000");
10.    }
```

```
11.     function resize1() {
12.       document.layers["interface_layer"].document.close();
        document.layers["interface_layer"].document.write("<IMG
        SRC=http://www.ruleweb.com/dhtml/Resize/interfac.jpg width=150
        align-left>");
13.     }

14.     </script>
15.     </head>

16.     <body bgcolor="black" onLoad="start();">

17.       <layer name="interface_layer" top=70 left=0 width=800
        height=300>
18.         <IMG SRC="http://www.ruleweb.com/dhtml/Resize/interfac.jpg"
        width=100 align=left>
19.     </layer>

20.     </body>

21.     </html>
```

Lines 16–19:

```
16.     <body bgcolor="black" onLoad="start();">

17.       <layer name="interface_layer" top=70 left=0 width=800
        height=300>
18.         <IMG SRC="http://www.ruleweb.com/dhtml/Resize/interfac.jpg"
        width=100 align=left>
19.     </layer>
```

Line 16 starts the script, executing the **start** function
(which we'll discuss shortly). The layer that is created,
interface_layer, contains the **interfac.jpg** image,
which has a width of 100 pixels. Notice that the layer must have a
width and height large enough to accommodate the largest size

that the image will attain. If you try to squeeze a 300-pixel-wide image into a 200-pixel-wide layer, the image will be clipped so that only part of it shows.

Lines 4–10:

```
4. function start() {
5. setTimeout(resize, "2000");
6. }

7. function resize() {
8. document.layers["interface_layer"].document.write("<IMG
   SRC=http://www.ruleweb.com/dhtml/Resize/interfac.jpg width=120
   align=left>");
9. setTimeout(resize1, "1000");
10.     }
```

The **start** function in line 4 simply waits 2 seconds (2,000 milliseconds) before executing the **resize** function. This wait is necessary so that the user sees the original image in the layer before the next one writes over it.

After 2 seconds, the **resize** function executes. It uses the **document.write** command to insert a new graphic into the **interface_layer** layer. The new graphic has a width of 120 pixels. The program then waits 1 second before executing the **resize1** function.

Lines 11–13:

```
11.     function resize1() {
12.     document.layers["interface_layer"].document.close();
   document.layers["interface_layer"].document.write("<IMG
   SRC=http://www.ruleweb.com/dhtml/Resize/interfac.jpg width=150
   align-left>");
13.     }
```

The **resize1** function first clears the layer by using the **document.close** function. Then it writes an image of its own—with a width of 150—into the layer. Although the functions stop here, you could continue them. You must remember, however, to clear out the layer before writing a new image.

Notice that we have inserted three of the same graphics with different widths (100, 120, and 150 pixels). We waited either 1 or 2 seconds between graphics, though these wait periods could be reduced to make the animation smoother. Unfortunately, in Netscape the transitions will always be jerky, because of the need to clear the layer before substituting another graphic.

SUMMARY

Resizing can be a nice effect if used in moderation. As we've seen in our examples, and particularly in the Netscape 4 demonstration, resizing of graphics in real time can produce poor results. Slow machines can be slow in resizing, and even fast machines can't overcome the pixelation that occurs when raster images (GIF, JPG) are resized.

The smoothest resizing that you will see on the web involves vector graphics. Vector graphics are used in Internet Explorer 5 in the Structured Graphics Active X control and in plug-in form in Macromedia's Flash. Until W3C picks a vector graphics standard, however, we will be stuck with resizing raster images. I would suggest using these techniques only where they can make a real impact.

PULL-DOWN AND POP-OUT MENUS

BACKGROUND

Web designers and developers have been waiting for pull-down and pop-out menus to appear on the web for years. Traditionally, they have had to deal with pull-down menus that existed as part of forms. These text menus have a number of design problems. First, they are rendered as text, so they size differently in different browsers and on different operating system. Nothing drives designers crazy like inconsistent layout. Second, the text menus look terrible from a designer's point of view. These problems have limited their use as navigational structures on the web.

Designers and web developers have really been looking for pull-down menus that are customizable and can be constructed from graphic elements. Users are very familiar with pull-down menus. Ever since the Macintosh computer came onto the scene in 1984, the pull-down menu has defined how hierarchical information is presented to the user. Until now, this familiarity has not extended to the web. Instead, navigational structure has been handled in many different ways. The most popular method was the left-side navigation bar that was first used by C|Net back when Netscape 1.2 initially came out. While this navigation structure has proved very popular, it provides no way to present deeper levels of information without loading a new page. Pull-down menus add an extra level of depth to sites and make this information available to the user without having to present it on a new page.

Users who have used pull-down menus on Macintosh, Windows 3.1, or Windows 95 systems feel comfortable with this navigation structure. This familiarity can be used to help novice users better navigate your site. In addition to providing the same functionality, the designer can use JavaScript to check the user's operating system and present a graphical design that is also familiar to the user. Having a Macintosh interface or a Windows 95 interface will make your site all the more familiar and accessible to the visitor.

Many sites make use of pop-out menus on their main pages. IBM (http://www.ibm.com), for example, uses a hierarchical menu to give a broad overview of its offerings. At Discovery, we use pop-out menus on the home page for Internet Explorer 4. One problem that we have at Discovery, and that all large web sites share, is exposing the depth of content found on the first page. Home pages for sites try to be both "magazine cover" and "table of contents" all on the same page. At Discovery, we use the pop-out menus to show many of our big stories from the last several weeks. This setup "drives" users down into the site and immerses them in our environment. Holding the user's attention and getting him or her to look at the full range of your product offerings represents one of the greatest challenges to today's web designers. Pop-out and pull-down menus are part of the solution.

Pop-Out Menus

These menus pop out from the side of the screen, almost always the left side. They are often represented by a tab that remains the only part showing until it is clicked on. The full menu is then revealed. Pop-out menus can be activated by several events, such as mouseovers, mousedowns, or onclicks. They can animate from the side of the screen or simply appear in their new locations. The pop-out menus illustrated in this chapter simply appear.

I'm not convinced that animation adds to the functionality. If you would like to add animation, however, you can use the cross-platform scripts in Chapter 9.

Pull-Down Menus

Pull-down menus are found in virtually all modern graphical operating systems. They are typically aligned across the top of the screen. When clicked on, they drop down to reveal more options.

TECHNICAL LIMITS

Menus work equally well in both Netscape and Internet Explorer browsers. You should not experience any technical problems.

The most important problem you will encounter derives from the visibility property of Cascading Style Sheet Positioning (CSS-P). Netscape uses the nonstandard **Hide** and **Show** parameters to determine visibility. Internet Explorer uses the W3C standard **Visible** and **Hidden** parameters. The scripts provided in this chapter work around this issue by using alternative scripts for the two browsers.

UNDERLYING TECHNOLOGY

Pull-down and pop-out menus are built around positioning and the event model. When one graphic is clicked on, then another appears. When the graphic is clicked on a second time, it disappears. A variable is set to 1 or 0 each time the image is clicked. This tactic keeps track of whether the menu should be hidden or shown.

EXAMPLES

The two examples in the remainder of this chapter are very similar; their only real difference is in direction.

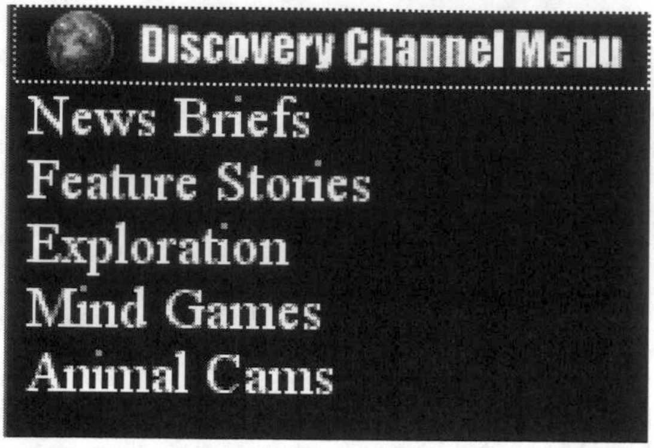

FIGURE 7-1.
Pull-down menu

Pull-Down Menu

This example simulates a pull-down menu from the Discovery Channel Online site (Figure 7-1). When you click on the menu bar, a selection of choices from the Discovery site is revealed. Listing 7-1 gives the code for this simulation (located at http://www.ruleweb.com/dhtml/Pull_Down_Menu/xplatform.html).

LISTING 7-1. PULL-DOWN MENU SIMULATION

```
1.  <html>
2.  <head>
3.  <title>Pulldown Menu</title>

4.  <script language="JavaScript1.2">

5.  if (document.layers) {n=1;ie=0}
6.  if (document.all) {n=0;ie=1}
7.  function init() {
8.     if (n) tab = document.tabDiv
9.     if (n) poptext = document.poptextDiv
10.    if (ie) tab = tabDiv.style
11.    if (ie) poptext = poptextDiv.style
12.    }

13.    var tabShow=1;
```

```
14.     //Hide-Show Layer
15.     function hidepoptext() {

16.     if (tabShow == 0) {
17.     if (n) {
18.     tab.visibility = "show";
19.     poptext.visibility = "hide";
20.     tabShow = 1;
21.     return;
22.     }
23.
24.     if (ie) {

25.     tab.visibility = "visible";
26.     poptext.visibility = "hidden";
27.     tabShow = 1;
28.     return;
29.     }
30.     }
31.     if (tabShow == 1) {
32.     if (n) {
33.     tab.visibility = "show";
34.     poptext.visibility = "show";
35.     tabShow = 0;
36.     }
37.     if (ie) {
38.     tab.visibility = "visible";
39.     poptext.visibility = "visible";
40.     tabShow = 0;
41.     }
42.     }
43.     }

44.     </script>

45.     <style>
46.     <!--
```

```
47.    #tabdiv {
48.    position:absolute;
49.    top:0px;
50.    left:0px;
51.    z-index:2;
52.    visibility:show;
53.    }

54.    #poptextdiv {
55.    visibility:hide;
56.    visibility:hidden;
57.    position:absolute;
58.    width:200px;
59.    top:15px;
60.    left:0px;
61.    z-index:0;
62.    color:white;
63.    border-color:black;
64.    border-width:2px;
65.    background-color:black;
66.    color:black;
67.    padding:10 5 10 5;
68.    z-index:1;

69.    }

70.    #maintext {
71.    position:absolute;
72.    top:10px;
73.    left:240px;
74.    width:470px;
75.    z-index:0;

76.    }-->
77.    </style>

78.    </head>
```

```
79.      <body onLoad="init()" bgcolor="White">

80.      <div ID=tabDiv>
81.      <a href="javascript:hidepoptext();"><img
         src="disnavbar.gif" width=200 height=25
         alt="" border="0"></a></div>

82.      <div ID=poptextDiv>
83.      <font size="+1" color="White">
84.      News Briefs<br>
85.      Feature Stories<br>
86.      Exploration<br>
87.      Mind Games<br>
88.      Animal Cams<br>
89.      </font>
90.      </div>

91.      </body>
92.      </html>
```

Listing 7-1 is one of the longer sequences of code that we've examined. If we divide it up, however, it becomes apparent that it's not as complicated as it looks.

Lines 5–12:

```
 5. if (document.layers) {n=1;ie=0}
 6. if (document.all) {n=0;ie=1}
 7. function init() {
 8.     if (n) tab = document.tabDiv
 9.     if (n) poptext = document.poptextDiv
10.     if (ie) tab = tabDiv.style
11.     if (ie) poptext = poptextDiv.style
12.     }
```

Lines 5 and 6 simply set up the browser detection. Line 5 says that if the document object model uses layers, then it must be a Netscape browser and **n** will be set to true.

Lines 7–12 execute when all HTML elements have been loaded. They remove some of the incompatibilities between Internet Explorer 4 and Netscape 4 by assigning browser-specific information to variables. This approach helps mask the DOM.

Line 13:

```
13.    var tabShow=1;
```

Line 13 creates the **tabShow** variable and sets it to 1, which means true. The **tabShow** variable keeps track of whether the pull-down menu is shown or hidden. When it is set to 1, the menu is hidden. Setting it to 0 will make the menu visible.

Lines 14–43:

```
14.    //Hide-Show Layer
15.    function hidepoptext() {

16.    if (tabShow == 0) {
17.    if (n) {
18.    tab.visibility = "show";
19.    poptext.visibility = "hide";
20.    tabShow = 1;
21.    return;
22.    }
23.
24.    if (ie) {

25.    tab.visibility = "visible";
26.    poptext.visibility = "hidden";
27.    tabShow = 1;
28.    return;
29.    }
30.    }
31.    if (tabShow == 1) {
32.    if (n) {
```

```
33.    tab.visibility = "show";
34.    poptext.visibility = "show";
35.    tabShow = 0;
36.    }
37.    if (ie) {
38.    tab.visibility = "visible";
39.    poptext.visibility = "visible";
40.    tabShow = 0;
41.    }
42.    }
43.    }
```

The **hidepoptext** function is the heart of the script. It contains two embedded **IF** statements, giving a total of four different states (Table 7-1).

TABLE 7-1. POSSIBLE STATES FOR THE **HIDEPOPTEXT** FUNCTION

State	Status
Netscape 4 and the **tabShow** variable set to 1	Pull-down menu is shown
Netscape 4 and the **tabShow** variable set to 0	Pull-down menu is hidden
Internet Explorer 4 and the **tabShow** variable set to 1	Pull-down menu is shown
Internet Explorer 4 and the **tabShow** variable set to 0	Pull-down menu is hidden

The **tabShow** variable acts as a switch that turns the menu from visible to hidden. This switch is accomplished with separate code for each browser by changing the "visibility" of the pop-text **DIV** area.

Lines 45–77:

The style sheet sets the characteristics of the pull-down menu. It is really just a **DIV** area with a black background. Listing 7-1 uses style sheets within their own **<style>** tags so that the style sheets will work across a variety of platforms.

Lines 80–81:

```
80.    <div ID=tabDiv>
81.    <a href="javascript:hidepoptext();"><img
       src="disnavbar.gif" width=200 height=25
       alt="" border="0"></a></div>
```

These lines specify the menu bar that you click on to trigger the pull-down menu.

Lines 82–90:

```
82.    <div ID=poptextDiv>
83.    <font size="+1" color="White">
84.    News Briefs<br>
85.    Feature Stories<br>
86.    Exploration<br>
87.    Mind Games<br>
88.    Animal Cams<br>
89.    </font>
90.    </div>
```

Lines 82–90 specify the pull-down menu that becomes visible. The text that appears here could easily be made linkable using a normal **<a href>** tag. You could also place a graphic within this **DIV** area and then apply an image map. The **DIV** tag is highly flexible; once you create it, anything can be put into it.

Pop-Out Menu

A pop-out menu, such as the one illustrated in Figure 7-2, is very similar to a pull-down menu. Instead of going over its code in detail (Listing 7-2, located at http://www.ruleweb.com/dhtml/popoutnetscape/popout.html), we will discuss its differences from the code for a pull-down menu.

FIGURE 7-2.
Pop-out menu

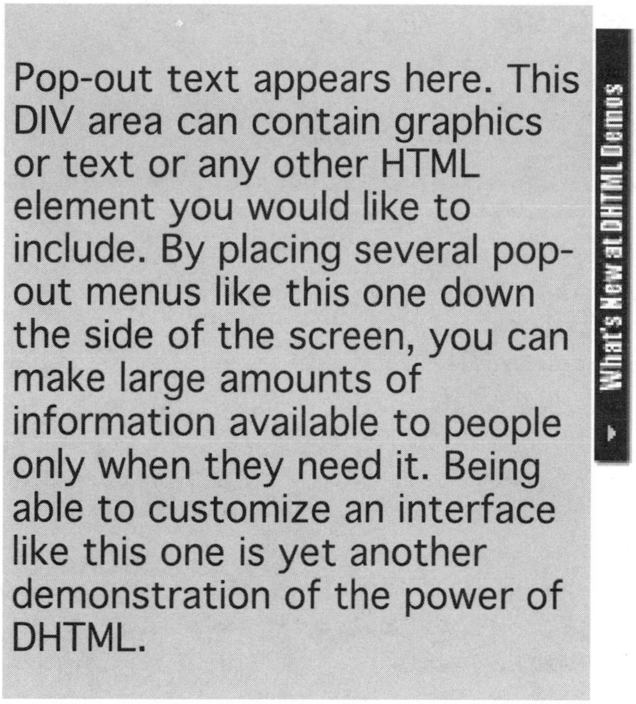

Pop-out text appears here. This DIV area can contain graphics or text or any other HTML element you would like to include. By placing several pop-out menus like this one down the side of the screen, you can make large amounts of information available to people only when they need it. Being able to customize an interface like this one is yet another demonstration of the power of DHTML.

What's New at DHTML Demos

LISTING 7-2. POP-OUT MENU SIMULATION

```
1.  <html>
2.  <head>
3.  <title>Popout Menu</title>
4.  <script language="JavaScript1.2">
5.  if (document.layers) {n=1;ie=0}
6.  if (document.all) {n=0;ie=1}

7.  function init() {
8.      if (n) tab = document.tabDiv
9.      if (n) poptext = document.poptextDiv
10.     if (ie) tab = tabDiv.style
11.     if (ie) poptext = poptextDiv.style
12.     }

13.     var tabShow=1;
```

```
14.     //Hide-Show Layer
15.     function hidepoptext() {

16.     if (tabShow == 1) {
17.     if (n) {
18.     tab.visibility = "hide";
19.     tab.left = 0;
20.     tab.visibility = "show";
21.     poptext.visibility = "hide";
22.     tabShow = 0;
23.     return;
24.     }
25.     if (ie) {
26.     tab.visibility = "hidden";
27.     tab.left = 0;
28.     tab.visibility = "visible";
29.     poptext.visibility = "hidden";
30.     tabShow = 0;
31.     return;
32.     }
33.     }

34.     if (tabShow == 0) {
35.     if (n) {
36.     tab.visibility = "hide";
37.     tab.left = 223;
38.     tab.visibility = "show";
39.     poptext.visibility = "show";
40.     tabShow = 1;
41.     }
42.     if (ie) {
43.     tab.visibility = "hidden";
44.     tab.left = 223;
45.     tab.visibility = "visible";
46.     poptext.visibility = "visible";
47.     tabShow = 1;
```

```
48.       }
49.       }
50.       }

51.       </script>

52.       <style>
53.       <!--
54.       #tabdiv {
55.       position:absolute;
56.       top:20px;
57.       left:223px;
58.       z-index:2;
59.       visibility:show;
60.       }

61.       #poptextdiv {
62.       visibility:show;
63.       position:absolute;
64.       width:223px;
65.       top:10px;
66.       left:0px;
67.       z-index:0;
68.       border-color:#000099;
69.       border-width:2px;
70.       background-color:#eeeeff;
71.       color:black;
72.       padding:10 5 10 5;
73.       z-index:1;
74.       }

75.       #maintext {
76.       position:absolute;
77.       top:10px;
78.       left:240px;
79.       width:470px;
```

```
80.     z-index:0;

81.     }-->
82.     </style>

83.     </head>

84.     <body onLoad="init()">

85.     <div ID=tabDiv>
86.     <a href="javascript:hidepoptext();">
87.     <img src="http://www.ruleweb.com/dhtml/
        popoutnetscape/tab.gif" width=15 height=164
        alt="" border="0">
88.     </a>
89.     </div>

90.     <div ID=poptextDiv>
91.     Pop-out text appears here. This DIV area
        can contain graphics or text or any other
        HTML element you would like to include. By
        placing several pop-out menus like this one
        down the side of the screen, you can make
        large amounts of information available to
        people only when they need it. Being able
        to customize an interface like this one is
        yet another demonstration of the power of
        DHTML.
92.     </div>

93.     </body>
94.     </html>
```

The main difference between the pop-out and pull-down menus is that the clicked-on graphic remains immobile in a pull-down menu, but moves in the pop-out menu. In the pop-out menu, the graphic serves as a tab that remains visible even when the menu choices are invisible.

The pop-out menu's tab graphic changes locations, jumping from **`tab.left = 223`** to **`tab.left = 0`**. This information is contained in the lines 19, 27, 37, and 44, which were not included in the pull-down menu code (Listing 7-1). Placing a number of these tabs along the edge of the screen is a great way to give users access to lots of information on one page.

SUMMARY

Content sites on the web are growing larger all the time. Sites such as those operated by Microsoft, IBM, and Netscape may contain thousands and thousands of pages. Many of them are buried so deeply that many users can never find them. Unfortunately, trying to place navigation aids to all this information on the home page or trying to squeeze it into a left-side navigation bar is impossible. In the future, these sites will be able to use pull-down menus and contextual pop-out menus to help users find the desired information. When access to information appears on the home page, the user doesn't have to dig as deep to find the targeted information.

At Discovery, we have noticed that the pop-out menus on the left side of the page allow us to direct users to older stories on the site. Typically, the Discovery main page features only four of our most current stories; by having older stories in the pop-out menus, however, we give our users access to the full range of older stories they may not have seen before.

Menus, whether pull-down or pop-out, represent an excellent way of presenting the user with a familiar navigation tool that helps to decrease clutter and make information more manageable.

LINKS

Internet Explorer 4 Examples

http://www.msnbc.com, http://home.microsoft.com
http://www.discovery.com (visible only with Internet Explorer 4+
    browsers)

Netscape 4 Examples

http://www.dhtmlzone.com/tutorials/index.html

DRAG AND DROP

BACKGROUND

As noted earlier, the web is making a transition from a page-based presentation to a stage-based format for interactive storytelling. Certain multimedia features make this transition easier, and the **drag-and-drop** feature is near the top of the list. Drag and drop is the basis for the two most popular operating systems on the market today: Windows 95/98 and the Macintosh operating system. In both of these operating systems, the user works with the desktop metaphor. He or she can drag icons around the screen, place them in folders, or drag them to the trash. The user is thus able to directly manipulate the objects on the screen, giving him or her a greater sense of control. With everything laid out on the desktop, the user has a graphical overview of all the necessary elements — nothing is hidden from the user.

Another underlying concept to the Windows and Macintosh operating systems is that all programs have a similar interface. On the Macintosh, pull-down menus have been displayed across the top of the screen since the release of the 1984 version of the operating system. The File menu always allows saving and closing, and the Edit menu always allows Cutting and Pasting. This consistency of interface gives an integrity to the operating system that makes users feel comfortable.*

Now let's compare this setup with the web. Every web page has a different interface, which the user has to figure out to navigate the site. There is no drag-and-drop feature. The user has no control over the web page. The page simply loads and is presented to the user, with no changes allowed.

When I originally came to web development from CD-ROM development, it was a tough change for me (not that CD-ROM had rigid design standards). I lost the ability to implement such features as drag and drop or to place pull-down menus at the top or bottom of the page. Without some sort of standardized interface for content, the web will have difficulty becoming a mass medium. Currently, it is a chaotic jumble of interfaces with no way to manipulate a page if you don't like its layout.

With Dynamic HTML, the user can retain some control over the page. Web developers can start to replicate the functionality that users see every day in their operating systems. For example, designers can let them drag icons around the screen again, so that users feel like they're in charge of this web space.

Always remember that the more comfortable a user is on your web site, the more likely that he or she is to buy from you or do whatever else your web page wants them to do. Nothing makes a user exit a page more rapidly than a confusing interface. In particular, drag and drop can help the user work with your web page more easily.

Shopping

E-commerce has been a buzzword on the web for the last year or so. Many of the current systems expect the user to keep items in a "market basket." Unfortunately, this market basket is invisible on most commerce pages. The user also must click on a link to place something in the basket.

With the advent of drag and drop on the web, we can now

---

*A great book to read for any interface developer is *Apple Human Interface Guidelines* (Apple Computer, Inc.).

more closely replicate the true shopping environment. Users can see a description of an item along with an icon representing it. If they are interested in the item, they merely drag it into their ever-present shopping basket. If they decide they don't want the item, they can put it back. Users don't even have to worry about putting the item back in the proper section of the store. (I bet you've ditched frozen peas in the ice cream section before.) This realistic approach to shopping more closely mimics the "real" shopping experience in the same way that the early Macintosh operating system closely mimicked the office desktop. This drag-and-drop approach is likely to become the standard interface for shopping sites once users upgrade to sufficiently powerful browsers.

Children's Games

Children (and many adults) love games and puzzles. Drag and drop offers a powerful new way to create these types of games on the web. Reportedly, a Dynamic HTML version of Risk, the game of world domination, is in the works. I've seen a number of sliding puzzle games in Dynamic HTML as well. There are also matching games where you must pick pairs of hidden pictures (see, for example, Shelley Powers' site at http://www.yasd.com/dynamicearth/games/pickpair.htm).

In addition to simple card and board games such as these, some people have taken the next step with Dynamic HTML and have started reproducing some of the early 1980s arcade games. Here are some examples:

Asteroids by Dan Steinman: http://drg.microsoft.com/dhtml/demos/asteroids/asteroids.htm

Tetris by Michael Wallent: http://drg.microsoft.com/dhtml/demos/HTMLtris/final.htm

Defender by Dan Steinman: http://members.xoom.com/dynduo/starthruster/ (Figure 8-1 shows this game in action.)

Drop and drag can be a powerful feature to add to any on-line game. It is especially useful in card games, puzzles, and matching games.

FIGURE 8-1. Star Thruster 2000 game

Test Taking

I spent several years developing computer-based training (CBT)
before moving to web development. My development tool of
choice was Macromedia's Authorware because of its excellent
testing components. Often testing consisted of multiple-choice
questions, but to make a truly immersive testing environment
we'd often use drag-and-drop testing. In this type of test, the user
would grab the proper icon or word and drag it into the answer
area. This action would then trigger a response, indicating either
a right or wrong answer. On a CD-ROM, this response was often
a movie giving more detail about the answer or explaining why

the user was incorrect. This drag-and-drop learning environment, although more difficult to program, received better feedback from testers. It kept them more interested and more involved in the test taking. Now that these features are available on the web, we may be able to leverage these lessons from the CD-ROM experience so as to make on-line quizzes as immersive as CD-ROM.

For an example of on-line quizzes using Dynamic HTML, try taking this quiz on the B2 Bomber that I produced for Discovery Channel at http://www.discovery.com/area/technology/b2/index.html (for Internet Explorer 4 users only).

Another example involves a human anatomy quiz that I prepared for Discovery Channel (but was never used). In this quiz, you must drag the bones to their correct place on the skeleton. Figure 8-2 shows this quiz, which is found at http://www.ruleweb.com/dhtml/Skeleton/skeletonheadworksx.html.

FIGURE 8-2.
Build a Skeleton quiz

Build a Skeleton

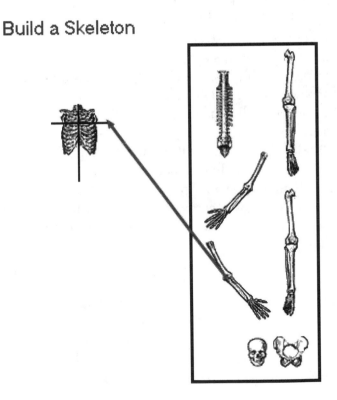

Controls and Interface Design

Replicating elements of the desktop in a browser window can be difficult and time-consuming. When completed, however, it provides an interface with which the user is already familiar. One effective drag-and-drop interface allows the user to drag an icon into an area to learn more about it. This "launch area" then brings up more information on the icon or launches a small browser window with more information. The drag-and-drop method is similar to dragging a file onto the main program file on a Macintosh or Windows 95/98 machine and launching the application with that file opened.

TECHNICAL LIMITS

Complicated drag-and-drop programs can be difficult to program in Dynamic HTML, especially in cross-browser format. Luckily, some development tools are extremely useful for creating complicated Dynamic HTML applications. The demonstrations in this chapter are relatively simple: They cause a single graphic to become draggable. If you intend to create a more complex application, such as the skeleton drag and drop from Figure 8-2, then you would be well advised to use an authoring tool. It's not that you can't create a cross-platform drag-and-drop application by coding it by hand—it's just that you can accomplish this task ten times faster in an authoring tool.

My authoring tool of preference is mBed Interactor from mBed Software. As discussed in Appendix A, this package is a full-fledged authoring tool that can output Dynamic HTML, Java, or its own proprietary format, which works with a plug-in. Drag and drop is especially easy in Interactor. After importing a graphic, you simply check a box to make it draggable. All of the necessary code is generated for you as output in formats compatible with Netscape 4 and Internet Explorer 4. You can also output Java for any Java-enabled browser.

Drag-and-drop playback should work well on any machine capable of running the version 4 browsers.

UNDERLYING TECHNOLOGY

Drag and drop is based on mouse-related events. **Events** are actions that the user takes, such as clicking or moving the mouse, resizing a window, or pressing a key. It may also include events that occur in the browser, such as onload for a window or an image. We will be dealing mostly with mouse events, such as mousedown, mouseup, and mousemove.

The new event models for JavaScript 1.2 provide much more awareness of what the mouse is doing. Previous event models didn't allow the detection of the *x, y* coordinates of the mouse. The combination of mousedown and mouseup events with this new detection of coordinates is what makes drag-and-drop applications possible in both browsers.

As with everything else, the event models for Netscape and Internet Explorer operate differently, especially in the creation of the event object. (See the Links section at the end of the chapter for sites that provide a more in-depth look at these event models.) Table 8-1 lists events for both browsers.

TABLE 8-1. EVENT MODELS

Netscape 4.0	Microsoft 4.0	What It Means
onClick	onclick	Single mouse click
onDblClick	ondblclick	Double mouse click
onDragDrop		When you drag an object (for example, a file) onto the navigator window
onKeyDown	onkeydown	When a key is pressed while typing in a browser document
onKeyPress	onkeypress	When any key is pressed
onKeyUp	onkeyup	When the key is released
onMouseDown	onmousedown	When the mouse button is clicked
onMouseMove	onmousemove	When the mouse is moved
onMouseOver	onmouseover	When the mouse is over an object
onMouseOut	onmouseout	When the mouse is no longer over the object
onMouseUp	onmouseup	When the mouse button is released

continued

TABLE 8-1. EVENT MODELS *(Continued)*

Netscape 4.0	Microsoft 4.0	What It Means
onMove		When the user or script moves a window or a frame
onResize		When the user or script resizes a window or frame
	ondragstart	When the user first begins to drag the selection
	onhelp	When the user presses the help key (F1)

EXAMPLES

The following sections provide examples of drag-and-drop code for Netscape and Internet Explorer browsers.

Netscape 4

Drag-and-drop code in Netscape 4 is based on three mouse events:

- A mousedown, initiated when the user selects the element to drag
- A mousemove, which detects the user's mouse movement
- A mouseup, initiated when the user releases the dragged element

These events and their relationships with a particular element (the graphic, in this case) form the basis for drag and drop. The element can be positioned anywhere on the page. The functions will grab this positioning number and use it in the calculations.

Listing 8-1 gives the code for this drag-and-drop operation.

LISTING 8-1. DRAG AND DROP IN NETSCAPE 4

```
1.  <!DOCTYPE HTML PUBLIC "-//W3C//DTD HTML 3.2 Final//EN">
2.
3.  <HTML>
4.  <HEAD>
5.      <TITLE>Drag and Drop Netscape 4</TITLE>
```

```
6.   </HEAD>
7.
8.   <STYLE TYPE="TEXT/CSS">
9.   <!--
10.     #iegear {
11.     position: absolute;
12.     left: 100;
13.     top: 100;
14.     layer-background-image: url(http://www.ruleweb.com/dhtml/
        preview/ns_gear.jpg);
15.     width: 82;
16.     clip: rect(0 82 82 0)
17.     }
18.     -->
19.     </STYLE>
20.     </HEAD>
21.     <BODY bgcolor="Black">
22.
23.
24.     <DIV ID="iegear"></DIV>
25.
26.
27.     <SCRIPT LANGUAGE="JavaScript1.2">
28.             <!--
29.
30.     currentX = currentY = 0;
31.
32.     function grabGear(gear) {
33.         currentX = gear.pageX;
34.         currentY = gear.pageY;
35.         captureEvents(Event.MOUSEMOVE);
36.         onmousemove = moveGear;
37.             }
38.
39.     function moveGear(gear) {
40.         distanceX = (gear.pageX - currentX);
41.         distanceY = (gear.pageY - currentY);
```

```
42.            currentX = gear.pageX;
43.            currentY = gear.pageY;
44.            document.iegear.moveBy(distanceX,distanceY);
45.                }
46.
47.    function dropGear() {
48.            releaseEvents(Event.MOUSEMOVE);
49.    }
50.
51.            document.iegear.document.onmousedown = grabGear;
52.            document.iegear.document.onmouseup = dropGear;
53.
54.            //-->
55.    </SCRIPT>
56.    </BODY>
57. </HTML>
```

Let's break down this code. In this example, we won't go in line-number order. Instead, we'll start with the mouse events and functions that form the core of this demonstration.

Lines 27–55:

```
27. <SCRIPT LANGUAGE="JavaScript1.2">
28.            <!--
29.
30. currentX = currentY = 0;
31.
32. function grabGear(gear) {
33.        currentX = gear.pageX;
34.        currentY = gear.pageY;
35.        captureEvents(Event.MOUSEMOVE);
36.        onmousemove = moveGear;
37.            }
38.
39. function moveGear(gear) {
40.        distanceX = (gear.pageX - currentX);
```

```
41.        distanceY = (gear.pageY - currentY);
42.        currentX = gear.pageX;
43.        currentY = gear.pageY;
44.        document.iegear.moveBy(distanceX,distanceY);
45.            }
46.
47.    function dropGear() {
48.            releaseEvents(Event.MOUSEMOVE);
49.    }
50.
51.            document.iegear.document.onmousedown = grabGear;
52.            document.iegear.document.onmouseup = dropGear;
53.
54.            //-->
55.    </SCRIPT>
```

In this case, the script must be below where the **DIV** tag containing the element appears. This is because the script applies to the element using the following command:

```
document.elementName.document.
onmousedown = functionName
```

This command cannot be carried out unless the element has been written to the screen. How can you grab the coordinates of an element that has not been put on the screen yet?

The first event the user initiates is to click the mouse on the element (the graphic, in this case) so as to drag it. In Netscape, this event is described as follows:

```
document.iegear.document.onmousedown =
grabGear
```

This command translates as "when the mouse button is pressed down on an element, a function is triggered." In our code, the mousedown event triggers the **grabGear** function. The **grabGear** function records the *x, y* coordinates of the element that was clicked on (in this case, the graphic of the gear). The coordinates are grabbed using the following lines:

```
currentX = gear.pageX;
currentY = gear.pageY;
```

The current *x* and *y* coordinates are set to the variables **currentX** and **currentY**.

The recording of these numbers in a variable triggers the **moveGear** function on a mousemove event. The **moveGear** function compares the new position of the element with its position on the page and recalculates its new position.

The graphic is finally released when the mouse button returns to the up position or is released. This event triggers the following command:

```
document.iegear.document.onmouseup =
dropGear;
```

When the element is released, the **moveGear** function stops calculating new positions and the element is left at its last position.

Lines 8–19:

```
8.    <STYLE TYPE="TEXT/CSS">
9.    <!--
10.      #iegear {
11.      position: absolute;
12.      left: 100;
13.      top: 100;
14.      layer-background-image: url(http://
         www.ruleweb.com/dhtml/preview/ns_gear.jpg);
15.      width: 82;
16.      clip: rect(0 82 82 0)
17.      }
```

```
18.        -->
19.        </STYLE>
```

Lines 8–19 define the element that will be moved. Most of this maneuver is set using the positioning that we learned in Chapter 3 (Cascading Style Sheets), but I want to point out one new technique. The graphic is defined in the following lines by making it the background of the **DIV** block:

```
layer-background-image:
url(http://www.ruleweb.com/dhtml/
preview/ns_gear.jpg);
```

This technique makes it easier to work with images in Netscape 4.

Internet Explorer 4

The code for drag and drop for Internet Explorer is somewhat different than the Netscape code, even though it follows the same pattern of mouse events. Remember that Internet Explorer mouse events are called differently than Netscape mouse events.

Here we use some of the same events, including **mouseDown**, **mouseUp**, and **mouseMove**. However, we add a new Internet Explorer 4-specific event called **ondragstart**.

Listing 8-2 provides the code for this drag-and-drop operation.

LISTING 8-2. DRAG AND DROP IN INTERNET EXPLORER 4

```
1. <HTML>
2. <HEAD>
3. <TITLE>Drag and Drop Internet Explorer 4</TITLE>
4. <SCRIPT LANGUAGE="JavaScript">
5. <!--
6. //set variables
```

```
 7. drag = 0
 8. move = 0

 9. function setDiv(dragger){
10. dragDiv=dragger
11. drag=1
12. }

13. function startdrag() {
14. window.document.onmousedown = mouseDown
15. window.document.onmouseup = mouseUp
16. window.document.onmousemove = mouseMove
17. window.document.ondragstart = mouseEnd
18. }

19. function mouseDown() {
20. if (drag==1) {
21. clickleft = window.event.x - parseInt(dragDiv.style.left)
22. clicktop = window.event.y - parseInt(dragDiv.style.top)
23. dragDiv.style.zIndex += 1
24. move = 1
25. }
26. }

27. function mouseEnd() {
28. window.event.returnValue = false
29. }

30. function mouseMove() {
31. if (move==1) {
32. dragDiv.style.left = window.event.x - clickleft
33. dragDiv.style.top = window.event.y - clicktop
34. }
35. }
36. function mouseUp() {
37. move = 0
38. }
```

```
39. //-->
40. </SCRIPT>
41. </HEAD>

42. <BODY onLoad="startdrag()" bgcolor="Black">

43. <!--Simply insert your image or text or whatever between the
    DIV tag-->

44. <DIV ID="gear" onMouseOver="setDiv(gear)"
    STYLE="position:absolute; left:200; top:200; width:90;
    height:90;">
45. <img src="http://www.ruleweb.com/dhtml/preview/ie_gear.jpg"
    width=90 height=90 alt="ie_gear" border="0">
46. </DIV>

47. </BODY>
48. </HTML>
```

Now let's analyze the code.

Lines 6–8:

```
6. //set variables
7. drag = 0
8. move = 0
```

Lines 6–8 initialize the variables for the script. When **drag** is equal to "1", then the **DIV** area that has been clicked on recalculates its position. The **move** variable is set equal to "1", and the recalculated numbers are used to update the **DIV** area's position.

Lines 9–12:

```
 9. function setDiv(dragger){
10. dragDiv=dragger
11. drag=1
12. }
```

The **setDIV** function allows the graphic that has been clicked on to become draggable. As we'll see later, this code can be used for any number of draggable objects on the page. In the example, we pass the **DIV** name "gear" to the function and make it equal to **dragDIV**. We also set **drag=1** so that the **mouseDown** function is now active.

Lines 13–18:

```
13. function startdrag() {
14. window.document.onmousedown = mouseDown
15. window.document.onmouseup = mouseUp
16. window.document.onmousemove = mouseMove
17. window.document.ondragstart = mouseEnd
18. }
```

After the HTML elements of the page are fully loaded, the **startdrag** function executes. It simply gives us simpler names for certain mouse events. This change makes these long strings easier to work with.

Lines 19–26:

```
19. function mouseDown() {
20. if (drag==1) {
21. clickleft = window.event.x - parseInt(dragDiv.style.left)
22. clicktop = window.event.y - parseInt(dragDiv.style.top)
23. dragDiv.style.zIndex += 1
24. move = 1
25. }
26. }
```

Lines 19–26 are where the true event capturing actually begins. Remember that we set **drag=1** back in line 11, so this function can now be executed. Lines 21 and 22 capture the position of the object when it is clicked on and pass it to two variables, **clickleft** and **clicktop**. The layer of the **dragDiv** graphic is also set to a higher value to ensure that it floats above the other objects on the page. The variable **move** is set to "1" so that the **mouseMove** function will work when we come to it.

Lines 27–29:

```
27. function mouseEnd() {
28. window.event.returnValue = false
29. }
```

This event is used to stop the return of position values after the user starts dragging the **DIV** area. If it is removed, the **DIV** area will follow the mouse around the screen even after the user releases the button.

Lines 30–35:

```
30. function mouseMove() {
31. if (move==1) {
32. dragDiv.style.left = window.event.x - clickleft
33. dragDiv.style.top = window.event.y - clicktop
34. }
35. }
```

These lines keep the position of the **DIV** area updated based on its current location and its original location. These calculations happen in real time and appear as the **DIV** area is being dragged. In many ways, this operation is similar to the calculated paths in animations (discussed in Chapter 9).

Lines 36–38:

```
36. function mouseUp() {
37. move = 0
38. }
```

When the mouse is released, the **move** variable is set to zero and the **mousemove** function stops calculating new positions.

In the body of the script, the **onload** event triggers the initial **startdrag** function in line 13. The graphic that we are dragging is contained in the **DIV** area called gear. When the mouse moves over the **DIV** area, this information is passed to the **setDIV** function that prepares this **DIV** area to be dragged.

This code is reusable and can be used to drag as many graphics as you'd like. You simply insert more **DIV** areas with different names and pass this information back to the **setDIV** function.

As an example, consider the following, which inserts another **DIV** area containing the Netscape 4 gear into the page and makes it draggable. Simply place this bit of code in your program **BODY**, and you're ready to go with two draggable objects.

```
<DIV ID="gear2" onMouseOver=
"setDiv(gear2)" STYLE="position:absolute;
left:300; top:300; width:90; height:90;">
<img src="http://www.ruleweb.com/
dhtml/preview/ns_gear.jpg" alt=
"ns_gear" border="0">
</DIV>
```

SUMMARY

Adding drag-and-drop functionality to your web pages is now within your reach. This powerful technique can be used to replicate some of the functionality of the graphical user interface from Windows 95/98 or Macintosh, or to develop a whole new interface. It is also great for developing games. I've used it at Discovery Channel to create games such as the Bolivia Animal game and the Build Your Own Rollercoaster game. The Rollercoaster game, in particular, brings a whole new level of game play to the Discovery site (Figure 8-3). Drag-and-match games such as these add a new dimension to gaming on the web. Classic matching games are especially great for interactive children's learning activities. Turn these new skills loose on your web page, and let me know what you create!

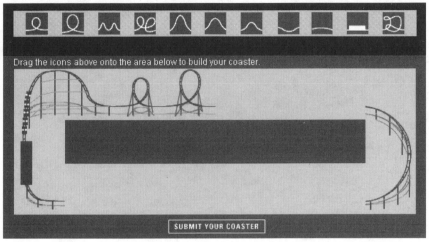

FIGURE 8-3. Rollercoaster game

LINKS

Games from Discovery Channel Online

http://www.discovery.com/exp/bolivia/game1.html

http://www.discovery.com/exp/rollercoaster/build.html

http://www.discovery.com/exp/antarctica/foodchain.html

DHTMLZone Article on Event Handling by Nick Heinle

http://www.dhtmlzone.com/articles/eventmodels.html

Microsoft Event Handlers

http://www.microsoft.com/msdn/sdk/inetsdk/help/dhtml/
doc_object/event_model.htm

Netscape Events

http://developer.netscape.com/library/technote/javascript/
   eventhandler/eventhandler.com and
http://developer.netscape.com/viewsource/
   goodman_drag/goodman_drag.html

ANIMATIONS

BACKGROUND

Animation is a trick. Dating back to the era of flip books and early movies, **animations** are a series of still images that appear in such rapid sequence that they give the illusion of motion. Television flashes these frames on the screen at a rate of 30 images per second. The frames appear and disappear so rapidly that the eye is tricked into thinking that the motion is smooth and continuous. Movies accomplish the same thing by presenting images at a rate of 24 frames per second (fps). If the rate slows to lower than 20 fps, the human eye starts to notice a jerky quality to the animation.

Dynamic HTML animation works in essentially the same way. The object, such as a graphic, must move somewhere between 24 and 30 times per second to give the illusion of smooth, continuous animation. For all its high-tech implementation, computer animation relies on the same tricks that early animators used to fool the human eye.

Animation is eye-catching. It adds life to dull web pages. After working with Dynamic HTML and its animation feature for more than a year, it's hard to believe that I was ever able to create compelling content for old browsers. Suddenly we've made the jump from displaying a pretty "picture book" to showing movies. Both are good at storytelling, if done properly, but movies are certainly more dramatic.

Until now, animation on the web could be done in only a few forms.

Animated GIF images are the most popular options, but they possess no interactivity. They are simply looping animations that rarely contain more than a few frames. In addition, they are confined to the "box" where they are positioned. When they are combined with Dynamic HTML animation techniques, GIF images can become quite compelling, allowing objects to both "travel" and "move" at the same time.

Shockwave, a plug-in from Macromedia, is one of my favorites. It is installed on an estimated 50%–75% of users' machines. Nevertheless, Macromedia continues to develop a Java implementation of Shockwave that should play in any Java-capable browser. Many of these Java-based Shockwave animations tend to run very slowly, however, and have large download sizes even for the most rudimentary animations.

Shockwave possesses a number of other drawbacks besides its plug-in architecture. File sizes are large even for non-Java versions. It must be remembered that Shockwave, produced by Director, was originally developed for CD-ROM. Even after two years of development, the Macromedia team is still trying to compress the files for Internet delivery. Once the files are delivered to the browser, they must run in the plug-in application. The Shockwave plug-in takes an additional 3MB of the user's RAM to run. With the already bloated browsers on the market, this capacity can exceed the 16MB of RAM that many users have installed.

One final blow against Shockwave is that it is confined to its box. Elements from the Shockwave movie cannot escape their box and interact with GIF images and text on the web page. Thus, while Shockwave is a great tool, Dynamic HTML is far smaller and has the advantage of being an integral part of the web page.

Java is a full-fledged programming language with many uses, including the creation of multimedia elements that are similar to Dynamic HTML. Programming animation in Java is considerably more difficult than similar programming in Dynamic HTML. In fact, it is nearly prohibitively expensive in terms of man-hours and difficulty. A number of good authoring tools for creation of animations on the web using Java are available, however. Liquid Motion (from Dimension X, recently acquired by Microsoft), for example, allows the creation of lightweight animations for the web. Interactor from mBed (discussed in Appendix A) is also a good tool. Interactor also allows the output of Dynamic HTML and Java from the same source file.

At Discovery, we have used Interactor to produce content that plays in Netscape 4, Internet Explorer 4, and Java-capable browsers. With this tool, we can author once and deliver the same content in multiple formats for the various browsers. Interactor Lite, which was recently released, can reduce the Java classes down to 30K, an acceptable download for web animation.

Java is best used for creation of web multimedia when universal playback is required. It tends to be larger in size, slower to start up, and more processor-intensive than Dynamic HTML.

Dynamic HTML breaks out of the mold by not being limited to a small window in the web page. Because they are included as part of the web page, animations created in Dynamic HTML are free to go anywhere on the page and interact with other elements. Dynamic HTML's only limits in providing web animation are its limit to the version 4 browsers and its inability to animate in three dimensions. Although it can change the layers of one object so that this image passes behind another object, it cannot make an object recede into the distance and shrink at the same time. Don't worry, though—the version 5 browsers will make this possible.

Types of Animations

Several different types of animation exist.

Point-to-Point Animation

A **point-to-point animation** travels along a straight line between two points. The number of points that it passes through along the way controls how smooth the animation appears. Point-to-point animations are normally calculated. In other words, the script causes the graphic to move by continuously adding 5 pixels to its distance from the left side of the screen. If this addition is done over and over again, the graphic will appear to move across the screen a few pixels at a time. If done rapidly enough, the motion will appear to be continuous. Calculated animations use a relatively large number of CPU cycles, as each new position must be calculated based on the last position.

Path Animation

To display animation along an irregular path, you must use path animation. **Path animations** read from a series of coordinates stored in the script to determine where the animated object should appear. Usually the script draws these numbers from a long string of numbers separated by commas. The individual coordinates are "parsed" from the string and used to reposition the object. This method is less computationally intensive than point-to-point animation because the numbers are already present in the code and don't need to be generated. An example of a path-based animation is the B2 Bomber demonstration at Discovery (located at http://www.discovery.com/area/technology/b2/mission.html and shown in Figure 9-1).

TECHNICAL LIMITS

Animations are fairly lightweight in terms of their demands on compute cycles and can play back even on slower computers. Calculated animations use more processor power than do animations that parse the coordinates from a string of numbers. Often the limiting factor for animations is the speed at which the screen refreshes. If the screen refreshes less frequently, the graphic may not redraw to the screen fast enough. The result is a jerky animation. Having many animations happening at the same time com-

> **TIP**
> ....
> Try to move only small objects. Larger objects take longer to redraw to the screen.

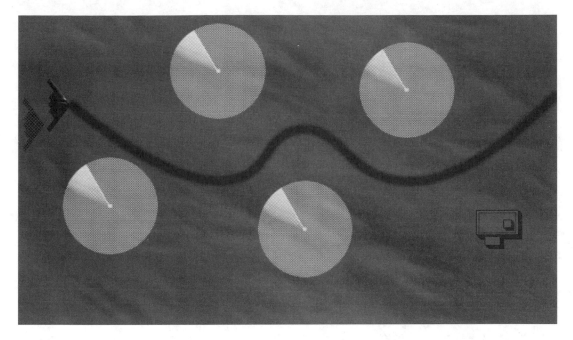

FIGURE 9-1. B2 Bomber animation path

pounds this problem. To assure good playback of animations, try to limit the number of objects moving at any one time.

UNDERLYING TECHNOLOGY

Animation is made possible by positioning HTML elements with Cascading Style Sheets (CSS-P). We discussed CSS-P back in Chapter 3. At the time, we did not differentiate CSS-P from CSS1. In the reality of today's web design, the two mingle together. In general, CSS1 controls the "look and feel" while CSS-P controls the positioning of objects on the screen. Animation in Dynamic HTML is possible because both of the version 4.0 browsers' DOMs allow the positions of HTML objects to be updated after they are written on the screen.

Let's briefly review the CSS parameters that make animation possible.

Positioning

Positioning is either absolute or relative.

Absolute positioning controls how far the HTML element is from the upper-left corner of the browser window.

Relative positioning controls how far the object is from its default position on the page. The default position is where the object would normally reside in the HTML layout.

Positioning is controlled by two parameters:

Left: The distance from the left edge of the browser window

Top: The distance from the top edge of the browser window

Z-Order

The Z-Order parameter controls the layering of the HTML elements. Images with higher Z-Order numbers appear to float above images with lower numbers.

Visibility

An HTML object is either visible or hidden. In Netscape 4, these states are called **Show** and **Hide**. In Internet Explorer 4, these states are called **Visible** and **Hidden**.

EXAMPLES

As we discussed earlier, there are two types of animations in Dynamic HTML: point-to-point and path animations. We will see two examples of point-to-point animations—one for Netscape 4.0 using layers, and one for Internet Explorer 4 that has a few extras beyond simple point-to-point animation. We will then examine a cross-platform example of path animation.

Netscape 4 Point-to-Point Animation

Listing 9-1 is a point-to-point animation for Netscape 4 found at http://www.ruleweb.com/dhtml/netscape/animation.html.

LISTING 9-1. NETSCAPE 4 POINT-TO-POINT ANIMATION

```
1.  <html>
2.  <head>
3.  <title>Example of Sliding Layers</title>

4.  <script language="JavaScript">

5.  function moveLayer(lyr,xadder,yadder,xend,timer) {
6.  lyr.top += yadder
7.  lyr.left += xadder
8.  if (((xadder > 0) && (lyr.left < xend)) ||
9.  ((xadder < 0) && (lyr.left > xend))) {
10. setTimeout('moveLayer(document.layers["'+lyr.name+'"],
    '+xadder+','+yadder+','+ xend +','+ timer+')',timer)
11. }
12. }

13. </script>

14. </head>
15. <body bgcolor="Black"
    onload="moveLayer(document.layers['ie_gear'],-4,-4,4,20)">
16. <layer name="ie_gear" top=100 left=100 visibility=show>
17. <img
18. src="http://www.ruleweb.com/dhtml/preview/ns_gear.jpg"
19. width=90 height=90 alt="IE4 Gear">
20. </layer>

21. </body>
22. </html>
```

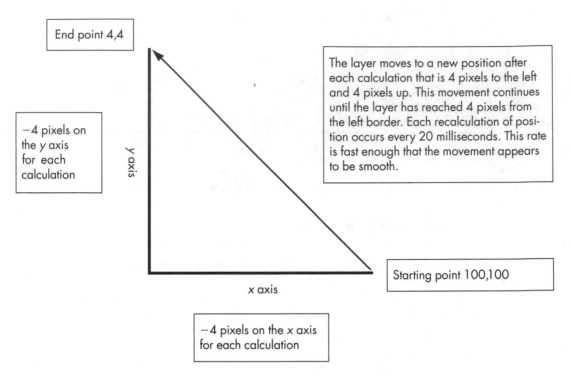

FIGURE 9-2. Calculation of a layer's end point

This example relies on a recalculation of the new position of the layer each time it moves. Because the graphic is contained in the layer, it moves along with the layer. In this example, we know the starting point. The end point must be calculated based on how much the layer moves during each operation. In each operation, the layer moves a certain distance along the *x* and *y* axes. Let's look at a calculation that can help us determine the end point. Figure 9-2 should look familiar to you if you took high school geometry.

With Figure 9-2 in mind, let's examine the code and see how we accomplish this recalculation.

Lines 4–13:

```
4. <script language="JavaScript">

5. function moveLayer(lyr,xadder,yadder,xend,timer) {
6. lyr.top += yadder
7. lyr.left += xadder
8. if (((xadder > 0) && (lyr.left < xend)) ||
9. ((xadder < 0) && (lyr.left > xend)))  {
10. setTimeout('moveLayer(document.layers["'+lyr.name+'"],
    '+xadder+','+yadder+','+ xend +','+ timer+')',timer)
11. }
12. }

13. </script>
```

This function is the engine behind the movement. It takes the raw numbers that you feed it and recalculates the position of the graphic. It continues to recalculate this position every 20 milliseconds until the graphic reaches a certain position on the *x*-axis—in this case, 4 pixels from the left margin. The function **MoveLayer** is passed five variables from line 15:

- **lyr**—The layer name (in this case, **ie_gear**)
- **xadder**—The amount the graphic is moved along the *x*-axis during each calculation (−4 pixels in this example).
- **yadder**—The same as **xadder**, but along the *y*-axis (also −4 pixels in this example)
- **xend**—The place on the *x*-axis where the function should stop recalculating the position and stop (4 pixels from the left margin)
- **timer**—The amount of time in milliseconds that the function should wait between recalculations (20 milliseconds)

In lines 6 and 7, the current position on the *x* and *y* axes has 4 pixels subtracted from it. The graphic moves from its original position at 100,100 pixels to 96,96 pixels in this first recalculation. The next recalculation will occur in 20 milliseconds.

Lines 8 and 9 check to see how the current position of the layer relates the **xend** position we entered (4) on the *x*-axis. Line 8 says that if **xadder** is a positive number (it's −4 in our demonstration) and the current position is less than the **xend** position, then the **moveLayer** function should execute again. Line 9 says that if **xadder** is a negative number (as in our example) and the current position is greater than the **xend** position, then the **moveLayer** function should execute again. The symbol | | means that if either of these statements is true, then the function should execute. The first statement is used if the layer is moving from left to right across the screen—that is, in a positive direction on the *x*-axis. The second statement is used if the layer is moving in a negative direction on the *x*-axis (as in our example).

If neither of these statements is true, then the function stops calculating new positions and the layer stops moving. If either one is true, then the **moveLayer** function is run in line 10.

Line 15:

```
15. <body bgcolor="Black" onload="moveLayer
    (document.layers['ie_gear'],-4,-4,4,20)">
```

Line 15 starts the execution of the **moveLayer** function. As you'll remember, the **onload** event occurs when all HTML elements on the page have finished loading. The **moveLayer** function is then triggered and passed the five variables (**lyr**, **xadder**, **yadder**, **xend**, and **timer**).

In line 15, you enter the values you want for the variables to make the animation move as desired. Try experimenting with different numbers in these positions and then look at Figure 9-2 to calculate how to do the point-to-point calculation.

Lines 16–20:

```
16. <layer name="ie_gear" top=100 left=100 visibility=show>
17. <img
18. src="http://www.ruleweb.com/dhtml/preview/ns_gear.jpg"
```

```
19. width=90 height=90 alt="IE4 Gear">
20. </layer>
```

This layer contains the **ie_gear** graphic. You can place any text or graphic you would like in this layer, and the code will move it. In fact, the **moveLayer** function can be used to move a layer of any name. All you need to change is the name of the layer that you pass to the function.

This Netscape 4 demonstration shows a simple way to move graphics or text around the screen. The code is very short and compact, and it can be reused for many different layers on the same page by changing the five variables (**lyr**, **xadder**, **yadder**, **xend**, and **timer**). Simple pieces of code such as this one can add flair to your web page without adding greatly to the total download time.

Internet Explorer 4 Point-to-Point Animation

The Internet Explorer 4 example differs slightly from the Netscape 4 example. In this example, the **DIV** area containing the graphic moves across the screen from left to right. Once it reaches a certain point, the graphic is swapped with another graphic. The new image then moves back across the screen from right to left. This bouncing behavior can be used on pages to create an ongoing animation. For example, you could use an animated GIF image of a man walking to the right. When he reaches the right edge of the screen, the image could be replaced by an image of a man walking to his left who strolls back across the screen. This animation would send the man pacing back and forth across your screen.

Our Internet Explorer 4 example is written in VBScript so that you can see its similarity to JavaScript. As we go through the code, I will point out some of the unique characteristics associated with VBScript, including one function that is not required for JavaScript.

Listing 9-2 provides the code for the Internet Explorer 4 point-to-point animation (found at http://www.ruleweb.com/dhtml/bounce/ie4_animation_book.html).

LISTING 9-2. INTERNET EXPLORER 4 POINT-TO-POINT ANIMATION

```
1.  <HTML>
2.  <HEAD>
3.  <TITLE>Point to Point and Back</TITLE>
4.  </HEAD>

5.  <script language=VBScript>
6.  dim count
7.  dim xadder
8.  dim yadder
9.  xadder = 5
10. yadder = 2

11. sub moveright
12. count=count+1
13. gearright.style.left = parseInt(gearright.style.left) + xadder
14. gearleft.style.left = parseInt(gearleft.style.left) + xadder
15. if (count<500/xadder) then
16. window.settimeout "moveright()", 100
17. else
18. count=0
19. gearleft.style.visibility="visible"
20. gearright.style.visibility="hidden"
21. window.settimeout "moveleft()", 100
22. end if
23. end sub

24. sub moveleft
25. count=count+1
26. gearleft.style.left = parseInt(gearleft.style.left) - xadder
27. gearright.style.left = parseInt(gearright.style.left) - xadder
28. if (count<500/xadder) then
29. window.settimeout "moveleft()", 100
30. else
31. count=0
32. gearleft.style.visibility="hidden"
```

```
33. gearright.style.visibility="visible"
34. window.settimeout "moveright()", 100
35. end if
36. end sub

37. function parseInt(rnum)
38. s=trim(rnum)
39. if len(s)>2 then
40. if right(s,2)="px" then
41. s=left(s,len(s)-2)
42. end if
43. end if
44. if isNumeric(s) then
45. i=csng(s)
46. else
47. i=0
48. end if
49. parseInt=i
50. end function

51. </script>

52. <BODY BGCOLOR="Black" onload="moveright()">

53. <img id=gearright style="position:absolute;left:0;top:80;
    z-index:1" src="http://www.ruleweb.com/dhtml/preview/
    ie_gear.jpg">

54. <img id=gearleft style="position:absolute;left:0;top:80;
    visibility:hidden;z-index:1" src="http://www.ruleweb.com/dhtml/
    preview/ns_gear.jpg">

55. </body>
56. </html>
```

As you look at the code in Listing 9-2, remember to compare it to JavaScript. It doesn't look very different, does it? Let's take this code apart.

Lines 6–10:

```
6. dim count
7. dim xadder
8. dim yadder
9. xadder = 5
10. yadder = 2
```

Lines 6–10 declare the variables that you will use in the script. The **dim** command creates the variables and then you assign values to them. Here we create **count**, **xadder**, and **yadder**:

> **count**—This variable is incremented by 1 each time the **moveright** or **moveleft** function executes. It is used to determine how many times to run these functions. In this example, **moveright** is run 500 times and then **moveleft** is run.

> **xadder**—As in our last example, this variable specifies the amount that the graphic is moved along the *x*-axis during each calculation.

> **yadder**—This variable isn't used in this example, but we'll discuss how it could be used. It is used the same way as in Listing 9-1.

Lines 11–23:

```
11. sub moveright
12. count=count+1
13. gearright.style.left = parseInt(gearright.style.left) + xadder
14. gearleft.style.left = parseInt(gearleft.style.left) + xadder
15. if (count<500/xadder) then
16. window.settimeout "moveright()", 100
17. else
18. count=0
19. gearleft.style.visibility="visible"
20. gearright.style.visibility="hidden"
```

```
21. window.settimeout "moveleft()", 100
22. end if
23. end sub
```

As its name probably gives away, this function causes the graphic to move from left to right across your screen. Notice that functions are declared using the word **sub** in VBScript instead of **function** and that no **{}** are used. In line 12, our **count** variable is increased by 1. This incrementing will happen every time that **moveright** is run until the number reaches 500; then **moveleft** will be run.

In lines 13 and 14, the positions of **gearright** and **gearleft** are increased by the amount contained in the variable **xadder** (in this case, 5). As only **gearright** is visible, we see only this graphic move. The other graphic is hidden, but still changing position!

Line 15 checks to see whether our variable **count** has reached 500 yet; if it has not, the **moveright** function continues to execute. Line 16 triggers the **moveright** function again after waiting 100 milliseconds.

The big moment happens in line 17. The script detects that **count** has reached 500 and executes what it should do if **count** is no longer less than 500. In this case, it sets the **count** variable back to zero, makes **gearleft** visible, and makes **gearright** invisible. Then it triggers the **moveleft** function.

We won't describe the **moveleft** function in detail because it is nearly identical to **moveright**. The only thing to notice is that the graphic is now moving from left to right. This movement occurs because **xadder** is now being subtracted from the position of the graphic. This function continues to execute until **count** reaches 500 and **moveright** is triggered. This cycle goes on forever.

Lines 37–50:

```
37. function parseInt(rnum)
38. s=trim(rnum)
```

```
39. if len(s)>2 then
40. if right(s,2)="px" then
41. s=left(s,len(s)-2)
42. end if
43. end if
44. if isNumeric(s) then
45. i=csng(s)
46. else
47. i=0
48. end if
49. parseInt=i
50. end function
```

VBScript is somewhat limited compared with JavaScript, as these lines demonstrate. The code contained in Listing 9-2 is used to convert the position of the graphic into an integer (a number) so that **xadder** can be added to or subtracted from it. This ability is built into JavaScript, so this bit of code would not be needed in JavaScript.

Earlier, we promised to demonstrate the use of **yadder** to change the position of the graphic on the y-axis. To use this variable, you need to add some code after line 14:

```
gearright.style.top =
parseInt(gearright.style.top) + yadder
gearleft.style.top =
parseInt(gearleft.style.top) + yadder
```

Notice that this code uses the **style.top** parameter to change the graphic's position on the y-axis. The amount by which it changes is controlled by the **yadder** variable, which we set to 2 at the beginning of the script. To make the graphic bounce, you also need to add code to the **moveleft** function after line 27. This code subtracts **yadder** from the graphic's y-axis position:

```
gearright.style.top =
parseInt(gearright.style.top) - yadder
```

```
gearleft.style.top =
parseInt(gearleft.style.top) - yadder
```

Using this extra code, you can create an example that moves on both the *x* and *y* axes and that creates a looping animation. In addition, you can swap the graphic so that a different one is used for each direction.

Cross-Platform Path Animation

We've seen two point-to-point demonstrations—one that works in Netscape 4 and another that works in Internet Explorer 4. When you are creating animations for the real world, however, it is nice to be able to create a single script that will play in both browsers. The script in the following cross-platform example is a path animation. As noted earlier, path animations are based on a series of coordinates that create a path for the animation to follow. They are much easier on the CPU than a calculated path, such as that employed in our two previous examples. Although I originally created this code as a path animation program, many viewers have also used it as a point-to-point animation. I will show you how to configure it to do both.

The demonstration uses the Internet Explorer 4 gear for the animation. Netscape users should feel free to use the Netscape gear. Nothing generates e-mail like using the Internet Explorer 4 logo in a Netscape demonstration! Never let it be said that programmers aren't passionate.

Let's look at the animation code, given in Listing 9-3.

LISTING 9-3. CROSS-PLATFORM PATH ANIMATION

```
1.  <HTML>
2.  <HEAD>
3.  <TITLE>Animation on Path</TITLE>
4.  <SCRIPT LANGUAGE = "JavaScript">
5.  bName = navigator.appName;
6.  bVer = parseInt(navigator.appVersion);
```

```
7.  if        (bName == "Netscape" && bVer == 4) ver = "n";
8.  else if (bName == "Microsoft Internet Explorer" && bVer == 4)
    ver = "ie";

9.  function init() {
10. if (ver == "n") {
11. pic = document.picDiv
12. pic.xcor = pic.left
13. pic.ycor = pic.top
14. }
15. else if (ver == "ie") {
16. pic = picDiv.style
17. pic.xcor = pic.pixelLeft
18. pic.ycor = pic.pixelTop
19. }

20. //Notice the first coordinate for the graphic is 64,74
21. pic.pathx = new Array(64,78,105,146,203,263,334,392,432,
    463,476,466,445,416,385,352,344,343,319,279,272,276,273,
    244,202,167,132,107,78,54)

22. pic.pathy = new
    Array(74,102,135,159,186,197,203,207,185,154,121,80,64,57,59,81
    ,109,138,153,140,114,89,53,43,42,45,54,35,26,52)

23. //Control Panel for Variables
24. pic.pathcor = 0           //don't change
25. pic.active = 1            // set to 1 to begin when page loads
26. pic.pathloop = 1          // set to 1 to loop, 0 not to loop
27. speed = .1                // time between points in seconds

28. picpath()}

29. function picpath() {
30. if (pic.active && pic.pathcor < pic.pathx.length) {
31. pic.xcor = pic.pathx[pic.pathcor]
32. pic.ycor = pic.pathy[pic.pathcor]
```

```
33. pic.left = pic.xcor
34. pic.top = pic.ycor
35. pic.pathcor += 1
36. setTimeout("picpath()",speed*1000)
37. }


38. else {
39. if (pic.active && pic.pathloop) {
40. pic.pathcor = 0
41. picpath()
42. }
43. else pic.active = 0
44. }
45. }


46. //-->


47. </SCRIPT>
48. <STYLE TYPE="text/css">
49. <!--
50. #picDiv {position:absolute; left:101; top:285; width:90;
    height:90;}
51. -->
52. </STYLE>
53. </HEAD>


54. <BODY onLoad="init()" bgcolor="Black" text="White">
55. <h3>Cross Platform Path Based Animation</h3>
56. <DIV ID="picDiv"><img src="http://www.ruleweb.com/
    dhtml/preview/ie_gear.jpg" width=90 height=90 alt="gear"
    border="0"></DIV>


57. </BODY>
58. </HTML>
```

Let's look at this code in detail.

Lines 5–8:

```
5. bName = navigator.appName;
6. bVer = parseInt(navigator.appVersion);

7. if       (bName == "Netscape" && bVer == 4) ver = "n";
8. else if (bname == "Microsoft Internet Explorer" && bVer == 4)
   ver = "ie";
```

These lines should look familiar to you from the discussion of compatibility issues in Chapter 1. Here we detect which browser the visitor is using and assign a code indicating the version: "N" for Netscape 4 and "IE" for Internet Explorer 4. We will use this code in the next area to sort out DOM incompatibilities.

Lines 9–19:

```
 9. function init() {
10. if (ver == "n") {
11. pic = document.picDiv
12. pic.xcor = pic.left
13. pic.ycor = pic.top
14. }
15. else if (ver == "ie") {
16. pic = picDiv.style
17. pic.xcor = pic.pixelLeft
18. pic.ycor = pic.pixelTop
19. }
```

The **init** function begins to execute as soon as all HTML elements are loaded to the page. This step is taken so that the animation doesn't start before the graphics are loaded. Having a blank graphical icon moving around the screen doesn't qualify as compelling content. We mask the DOMs, and we place the *x* and *y* positions of the **picDiv** graphic in the **pic.xcor** and **pic.ycor** variables, respectively. The functions can then work with the positions regardless of which browser is used to view the page.

Lines 20–22:

```
20. //Notice the first coordinate for the graphic is 64,74
21. pic.pathx = new Array(64,78,105,146,203,263,334,392,432,463,
    476,466,445,416,385,352,344,343,319,279,272,276,273,244,202,
    167,132,107,78,54)

22. pic.pathy = new Array(74,102,135,159,186,197,203,207,185,154,
    121,80,64,57,59,81,109,138,153,140,114,89,53,43,42,45,54,35,
    26,52)
```

As noted earlier, path animations are made from a series of points that the graphic jumps between. If the jumps are small and happen very quickly, the human eye perceives them as a smooth movement. If the graphic jumps approximately 20 pixels at a time and it happens slowly, the animation will look jerky. Lines 21 and 22 contain the points along the path. Line 21 contains the *x* coordinates, or the distance of the graphic from the left side of the screen. Line 22 contains the *y* coordinates, or the distance of the graphic from the top of the screen.

These numbers are contained in a JavaScript element called an array. An **array** holds long lists of items that then can be taken out of the array in order. In this case, the functions will pick the *x* and *y* coordinates out of these arrays to position the graphics during the animation.

The position of the first point in the animation is 64,74. These numbers are the first entries in the two arrays.

Lines 23–28:

```
23. //Control Panel for Variables
24. pic.pathcor = 0              //don't change
25. pic.active = 1              // set to 1 to begin when page loads
26. pic.pathloop = 1           // set to 1 to loop, 0 not to loop
27. speed = .1                 // time between points in seconds

28. picpath()}
```

Lines 23–28 are the "control panel" for the script; they contain many of the variables that you will need to control the animation.

Line 24: Don't change this number. **pic.pathcor** controls the number being picked out of the array. It will be incremented by 1 each time that the **picpath** function executes.

Line 25: The **pic.active** variable controls whether the script starts when the page loads. If it is set to 1, the script will begin when the page loads. If **pic.active** is set to 0, then it will need to be triggered some other way.

Line 26: The **pic.pathloop** variable controls the looping of the animation. If it is set to 1, the program loops infinitely. If it is set to 0, the program will play only once.

Line 27: I got tired of calculating everything in milliseconds, so I modified the script. In this example, the graphic moves to its next point in the path animation every .1 seconds.

Line 28: This line triggers the **picpath** function, which uses all of the variables that we've been setting.

Lines 29–45:

```
29. function picpath() {
30. if (pic.active && pic.pathcor < pic.pathx.length) {
31. pic.xcor = pic.pathx[pic.pathcor]
32. pic.ycor = pic.pathy[pic.pathcor]
33. pic.left = pic.xcor
34. pic.top = pic.ycor
35. pic.pathcor += 1
36. setTimeout("picpath()",speed*1000)
37. }

38. else {
39. if (pic.active && pic.pathloop) {
```

```
40. pic.pathcor = 0
41. picpath()
42. }
43. else pic.active = 0
44. }
45. }
```

Lines 29–45 code the controlling function of the script. This function pulls the coordinates from the array one by one and moves the graphic to these coordinates.

Line 30: Here we check whether both **pic.active** and **pic.pathcor** are less than **pic.pathx.length**. What does that really mean? The **pic.pathcor** variable is increased by 1 every time the function executes. The **pic.pathx.length** variable is the number of *x* coordinates given in line 21. If you count them, you'll see that this animation includes 30 points. This statement ensures that once 30 coordinates have been picked from the arrays, the function stops and doesn't try to grab more coordinates than it has.

Line 31: Here we grab the first *x* coordinate from the array. The **[pic.pathcor]** argument determines the number being picked.

Line 32: This line does the same for the *y* coordinate.

Lines 33 and 34: The new coordinates from the array become the position of the graphic. The graphic actually moves at this point.

Line 35: **pic.pathcor** is incremented by 1 and the **picpath** function recommences after waiting 10 milliseconds.

Lines 38–43: These lines control what happens after **pic.pathcor** becomes equal to 30 and there are no more coordinates to pull from the array. If **pic.active** is set to 1 and **pic.pathloop** is set to 1, then the function will set **pic.pathcor** back to 0 and restart the function. If either `pic.active` or `pic.path` is not set to 1, the function will end.

In the body of the document, the **DIV** area contains the graphic of the Internet Explorer gear. You can place any graphic or any text you want into this **DIV** block, and it will be moved along the path you set up.

Where can you get the coordinates to create this path? The best course of action is to plot them out in Photoshop or some other program that tells you the coordinates as you run your mouse over the screen. Try to keep your coordinates evenly spaced, or the graphic will appear to lurch drunkenly around the screen.

SUMMARY

This chapter may not prepare you to work as an Imagineer for Disney, but it's a start. Its lessons will allow you to accomplish things on a web page that simply weren't possible until recently. As Dynamic HTML currently exists, animation can be done in only two dimensions. Having the object pass behind other objects can simulate the third dimension, but true three-dimensional animation is not possible. In the future, browsers may permit "depth of field" operations, so that objects become smaller as they retreat into the distance and larger as they come closer to the viewer. We will then begin to see true television-style animation on the web.

LINKS

Another Animation Script

http://www.webcoder.com/howto/article.html?number=10, length=6,demo=1,source=1

Animation Development Techniques

http://developer.netscape.com/docs/manuals/tools/devguide/ devtech.htm#1013897

Cascading Style Sheet Positioning

http://developer.netscape.com/viewsource/angus_css.html

TIMELINES AND SEQUENCING

BACKGROUND

As we discussed earlier, web development is moving from page- to stage-based content. Page-based content loads all at once along with the page itself and then remains constant. Stage-based content loads over time; it is choreographed and continually changing. New content does not need to be introduced by opening a new page—it can be loaded "offstage" and then made visible only when needed. Content that is no longer needed can be made invisible and sent "offstage." This ongoing action gives Dynamic HTML developers new ways to express themselves that are closer to CD-ROM development than traditional web development (assuming that something with a three-year history can actually have "traditions").

The **timeline** is the master script that controls the other scripts we have discussed to this point. Its importance cannot be overemphasized. Without it, web pages take place at one instance in time; with it, the pages are transformed into content that unfolds in front of the user, drawing the user into the content, setting mood, introducing ideas, and developing them. The timeline is the script that tells the other functions when to act.

155

Let's walk through an example showing what you could accomplish with this type of control script and some of the other scripts we've discussed.

Page Loads: The title graphic fades in using transitions (see Chapter 5). It holds for 2 seconds and then fades out.

3 Seconds: A splash screen comes up using animations (see Chapter 9) to introduce the content. An animated story plays and then fades out.

8 Seconds: The main content loads after being introduced by a title and a splash screen. This content consists of text, graphics with filters applied, pull-down menus, and drag-and-drop examples.

All of this activity appears on the same web page. There is no need to load new pages to see new information; this is the main difference between page- and stage-based web content. It is the future of the web, too.

> **T I P**
> ....
> (For Macromedia Director users) The timeline we will discuss in this chapter is much like the Score in Macromedia Director. It is more limited in its ability to jump around than the Score, but provides the same time-based presentation of content.

UNDERLYING TECHNOLOGY

The two scripts described in detail in this chapter perform exactly the same function, but are based on very different technologies. We have attempted to keep the terminology as close as possible between these two scripts, however. The naming conventions are borrowed from the Active X object for the cross-browser JavaScript, so, for example, each time point is associated with a "Seq" command that means "Sequence."

Cross-Browser JavaScript

The only truly cross-platform language is JavaScript, which is used in both Internet Explorer 4 and Netscape 4. It is also the only language supported in Internet Explorer for Macintosh and UNIX. Microsoft has chosen not to support VBScript or Active X in its launch of Internet Explorer on these platforms.

The first example in this chapter is a timeline built in cross-platform JavaScript. It works equally well in Internet Explorer 4 and Netscape Communicator 4. Its power lies in its simplicity and ease of use. The only changes that you will need to make to the script affect a few lines, making it easy to configure. The script avoids any of the DOM conflicts between Internet Explorer 4 and Netscape 4.

Active X and VBScript

You might ask why the second script based on Active X and VBScript is even necessary. If anything, the Active X object is even easier to configure then the JavaScript object. If you are working in Internet Explorer 4 for the PC environment, I would reluctantly say that you should use the Active X/VBScript combination instead of JavaScript. If you are creating code that will be ported to Netscape or viewed with Internet Explorer 4 or UNIX, then you should use the JavaScript—you will have far fewer conflicts in your porting.

As discussed in Chapter 11, some Active X components are built into Internet Explorer 4 for PC. Many of these components were built to make the developer's job much easier. One of these components is the sequencing object. The sequencing Active X object allows the developer to create a timeline for the web page. You may remember that a timeline was one of the key steps in the progression from page- to stage-based web media. This Active X object is easy to configure because it doesn't have any functions. It is simply a parameter that you change, perhaps indicating the time that the function should execute and which function should execute. There are no functions because the parameters are passed to the Active X object, which you never need to worry about. The Active X object is controlled by a few simple, easy-to-understand lines of VBScript. It's an elegant solution, but it runs on only one browser. I recommend using this script only in an intranet environment where the users are standardized on Internet Explorer 4 for PC or where a separate area is set aside for users of Internet Explorer 4 for PC.

In addition to being easier to configure, the Active X object also allows you to pause, stop, and loop the execution of functions. Also, much like Macromedia Director, it allows you to jump around the timeline so as to reuse functions. We'll go into greater detail regarding these functions in the "Examples" section.

Performance Issues

Active X objects aren't nearly as efficient as scripts. They are additional components that need to be loaded into memory. As such, they require memory that some older computers may be hard-pressed to provide. Developers need to take this issue into account when choosing Active X rather than JavaScript. To overcome this problem, you can set up multiple timelines that operate independently of one another. These timelines are called Action Sets in Microsoft-speak. Having a single action set is the most efficient way to handle performance-related issues. If you need two action sets, it is best to use two sequences from the same Active X object. The least effective way to handle this problem is to load multiple Active X objects into memory.

The sequence control can also perform very differently on machines with different setups. If the developer makes a call that triggers an animation when the page is loading, the animation may take different amounts of time to run on various machines. Thus it is hard to time another function to start when the first animation is supposed to end. One way to circumvent this issue is to have multiple timelines, with only one function included in each timeline. When one action ends, you can tell the next action to start. This strategy avoids the timing issues.

EXAMPLES

First, we'll look at the JavaScript example. Then we'll turn to the Active X and VBScript script.

JavaScript

Let's dissect this JavaScript code and discuss how it can be used to make time-based events happen on the web.

Listing 10-1 is stripped down to the basics. It fires a JavaScript alert message every few seconds. (Alert messages are those annoying boxes that pop up occasionally, usually when you have an error.) In our example, each alert box indicates which function has just been triggered by the timeline script.

LISTING 10-1. JAVASCRIPT SEQUENCING

```
1.  <HTML>
2.  <HEAD>
3.  <TITLE>Sequencing</TITLE>

4.  <!--Substitute your functions here-->

5.  <script language="JavaScript1.2">
6.  function function1()
7.  {
8.  window.alert("Function1 at Load")
9.  }

10. function function2()
11. {
12. window.alert("Function2 at Load also")
13. }

14. function function3()
15. {
16. window.alert("Function3 at 1.5 seconds")
17. }

18. function function4()
19. {
20. window.alert("Function4 at 5 seconds")
21. }
22. </script>

23. <!--End Substitute Your Functions-->

24. <!--These are the Sequence Functions -->
25. <SCRIPT LANGUAGE = "JavaScript">
```

```
26. //don't change
27. function startSeq(SeqNumber) {
28. Time[SeqNumber] = 0;
29. SeqController(SeqNumber);
30. }

31. //don't change
32. function stopSeq(SeqNumber){
33. Time[SeqNumber] = Seq[SeqNumber].length;
34. }

35. //don't change
36. function SeqController(SeqNumber) {
37. if (Time[SeqNumber] <= Seq[SeqNumber].length - 1) {
38. Time[SeqNumber]++;
39. if (Seq[SeqNumber][Time[SeqNumber]] != null){
40. eval(Seq[SeqNumber][Time[SeqNumber]]);
41. }
42. setTimeout('SeqController(' + SeqNumber + ')', 100);
43. }
44. }

45. //don't change
46. function init() {
47. Time = new Array();
48. Seq = new Array();

49. // Don't change. Seq starts here.
50. Seq[0] = new Array();

51. // Change. After one second has passed
    (note the 10 in the second bracket), trigger functions 1 and 2.
52. Seq[0][10] = 'function1(); function2();';

53. // Change. After 1.5 seconds (from the beginning),
    trigger function 3.
54. Seq[0][15] = 'function3();';
```

```
55. // Change. After 5 seconds, trigger function 4.
56. Seq[0][50] = 'function4();';

57. //don't change
58. startSeq(0);
59. }

60. var totalTime, currTime;
61. var Time, Seq;

62. </SCRIPT>
63. </HEAD>
64. <BODY onLoad = "init()">
65. <font face="Arial Black" size="+2" color="Red">This is a very
    powerful script</font><p> This is a sequencing script written
    to trigger functions at different times.  For those of you
    familiar with the Sequencing Active X Object built into IE4,
    you'll love this. One of the main strengths of Dynamic HTML is
    the ability to have action take place over time.  With this
    script you can trigger an animation when the document loads,
    then at 3 seconds have a title appear.  At 5 seconds, the title
    disappears and the main screen loads. This script is cross-
    platform for IE4 and NS4. Those of you who want to support IE4
    Mac and IE4 UNIX will need to use this script instead of the
    Sequencing Object because IE4 Mac and UNIX won't support Active
    X. An example of the Sequencing Object can be found in the
    Sequence Active X.
66. </BODY>
67. </HTML>
```

You can see this code in action on the accompanying web site at: http://www.ruleweb.com/dhtml/sequence/sequence.html.

Listing 10-1 can be broken down into three different sections.

Section 1. This area contains the functions that the timeline script should execute. These functions can be ones you've written on your own, or they can be functions discussed earlier in this book. Try inserting a function that triggers a graphic to fade up here. The demonstration includes four functions that pop up alert messages. These alert messages indicate which function has just executed and the time at which it executed.

Section 2. The first half of the sequence comprises a number of functions you don't need to touch because they control the timing. These functions are marked with comments saying "don't change." The second half of the sequence area is marked "change." Here you can specify when the functions will execute and which functions should execute.

Section 3. The third section is the body of the document, with which you are already familiar. You place the graphics and text that the functions control in this section.

Section 1
Lines 5–23

First, you must plug in your own functions. In this example, we have simply substituted a number of alert window pop-ups. These simple functions are triggered by the timeline script. In your real-world script, you would replace the alert functions, such as

```
8. window.alert("Function1 at Load")
```

with a useful function such as one that makes a graphic invisible,

```
pic1.style.visibility="hidden"
```

Using this technique, you can make objects appear and disappear over time in a choreographed manner. All you need to do is to swap out the alert box functions with other functions you'll find in this book.

Section 2

Part A (Lines 24–50)

These functions should not be changed. They control the sequence and keep track of which part of the sequence is being executed.

Part B (Lines 51–56)

This part of the script controls the times at which certain functions are executed. It is the heart of the script. Here you can control the time points and set the flow of your stage-based presentation. Let's look at the first time point and examine it in detail:

```
52. Seq[0][10] = 'function1();
function2();';
```

In sequence 0, at 1 second (10 represents 1 second; 20 is 2 seconds; and so on) both function 1 and function 2 are executed.

You may also set up multiple timelines by replacing 0 with a number, as shown below:

```
52. Seq[1][10] = 'function1();
function2();';
```

With this change, you have set up two timelines that run simultaneously. This approach can be useful for organizing information. Timeline 1 can control graphics, for example, while timeline 2 controls text.

Section 3

Lines 64–67

This area contains the body of the document, where you will place the graphics and text that the functions will control. Notice that the timeline script is triggered in line 64 by the **onLoad** event. This event ensures that all graphics and text have finished loading before the timeline starts. You wouldn't want broken images moving around the screen in a choreographed manner!

Active X and VBScript

Active X is a very different technology than JavaScript, but in the end it accomplishes the same thing. Active X controls can be thought of as small helper applications, in some ways much like plug-ins that add functionality to the browser. Unlike plug-ins, Active X controls can be automatically downloaded over the Internet when needed. Many Active X controls, such as Macromedia's Shockwave control, exist both as Active X components and as plug-ins. The Sequencer control is slightly different from these controls in that it is built into the browser and does not need to be downloaded. Having this powerful functionality greatly increases what you can do with the browser, but it also limits your programs' compatibility with other browsers that don't support Active X.

With the limitations of Active X, you might wonder, "Why not just use JavaScript?" As noted earlier, Active X adds looping, pausing, and stopping functions and it permits jumping around on the timeline. Listing 10-1, in contrast, does not contain the same functionality as the Active X Sequencer control. We'll begin with the basics of how to use this object (just as we did with the JavaScript example), and then we'll show some of its more complex features.

Listing 10-2 is based on demonstrations from the site called Active X Sequence. It uses the sequence control to apply transitions to three images in an even more straightforward manner than is possible in the JavaScript sequencer.

Here's a walkthrough of what is happening in Listing 10-2:

Lines 6–8: The sequence 1 Action Set begins to play as soon as the page is loaded.

Line 10: Sequence 1 at 1 second executes the `pic1_show` function, which applies a filter to `pic1` that makes it visible through a fade over a period of 2.5 seconds.

Line 11: **pic2** is shown at 3 seconds after the page is loaded by a fade-up over a period of 1.4 seconds.

Line 12: **pic1** fades back out at 6 seconds by a fade that lasts 2.5 seconds.

Line 13: **pic3** is made visible at 8 seconds by a wipe-down that lasts 1 second.

Line 14: **pic2** is hidden again by a fade at 10.2 seconds.

Line 15: **pic3** is hidden at 11.1 seconds by a down-wipe that lasts 1 second.

You may have noticed the cryptic string of numbers and letters near the end of the script:

```
<OBJECT ID="Seq" CLASSID="CLSID:
B0A6BAE2-AAF0-11d0-A152-00A0C908DB96">
</OBJECT>
```

This string is how the browser knows that you are using the Active X sequencing object in this script. **CLASSID** is merely an identification string. Rumor has it that putting the Active X object at the end of your script enhances performance because everything else is loaded first. Although I can't confirm this claim, I always write my programs this way for consistency.

Now let's look at Listing 10-2 in detail.

LISTING 10-2. ACTIVE X SEQUENCING

```
1. <HTML>
2. <HEAD>
3. <TITLE>Sequence</TITLE>
4. <SCRIPT LANGUAGE="VBSCRIPT">
5. <!--
6. Sub Window_onload()
7. Call Seq("1").Play
8. End Sub
```

```
 9. Sub Seq_OnInit()
10. Call seq("1").at(1.000, "pic1_show", 1, 0.000, 1)
11. Call seq("1").at(3.000, "pic2_show", 1, 0.000, 1)
12. Call seq("1").at(6.000, "pic1_hide", 1, 0.000, 1)
13. Call seq("1").at(8.000, "pic3_show", 1, 0.000, 1)
14. Call seq("1").at(10.200, "pic2_hide", 1, 0.000, 1)
15. Call seq("1").at(11.100, "pic3_hide", 1, 0.000, 1)

16. End Sub

17. Sub pic1_show()
18. pic1.filters(0).apply()
19. pic1.style.visibility = "visible"
20. pic1.filters(0).play()
21. End Sub

22. Sub pic2_show()
23. pic2.filters(0).apply()
24. pic2.style.visibility = "visible"
25. pic2.filters(0).play()
26. End Sub

27. Sub pic1_hide()
28. pic1.filters(0).apply()
29. pic1.style.visibility = "hidden"
30. pic1.filters(0).play()
31. End Sub

32. Sub pic3_show()
33. pic3.filters(0).apply()
34. pic3.style.visibility = "visible"
35. pic3.filters(0).play()
36. End Sub

37. Sub pic2_hide()
38. pic2.filters(0).apply()
39. pic2.style.visibility = "hidden"
40. pic2.filters(0).play()
41. End Sub
```

```
42. Sub pic3_hide()
43. pic3.filters(0).apply()
44. pic3.style.visibility = "hidden"
45. pic3.filters(0).play()
46. End Sub
47. -->
48. </SCRIPT>

49. <style>
50. #pic1 {
51. position: absolute;
52. top: 1;
53. left: 1;
54. }

55. #pic2 {
56. position: absolute;
57. top: 150;
58. left: 150;
59. }

60. #pic3 {
61. position: absolute;
62. top: 200;
63. left: 300;
64. }
65. </style>

66. </HEAD>

67. <BODY topmargin="0" leftmargin="0" bgcolor="#FFFFFF">

68. <CENTER>

69. <IMG id="pic1" SRC="image2/1.jpg" WIDTH=300 HEIGHT=408 BORDER=
    "0" style="position: absolute; left: 100; top: 100; z-index:
    1; visibility: hidden; filter:blendTrans(duration=2.50)">
70. <IMG id="pic2" SRC="image2/2.jpg" WIDTH=300 HEIGHT=207 BORDER=0
    style="position: absolute; left: 200; top: 150; z-index: 1;
    visibility: hidden; filter:blendTrans(duration=1.4)">
```

```
71. <IMG id="pic3" SRC="image2/3.jpg" WIDTH=300 HEIGHT=238 BORDER=0
    style="position: absolute; left: 350; top: 200; z-index: 1;
    visibility: hidden; filter:revealTrans(duration=1.0,
    transition=5)">
72. <OBJECT ID="Seq" CLASSID=
    "CLSID:B0A6BAE2-AAF0-11d0-A152-
    00A0C908DB96">
73. </OBJECT>

74. </CENTER>

75. </BODY>

76. </HTML>
```

That's the basics of the script. The numbers after the sequence,

```
Call seq("1").at(1.000, "pic1_show",
1, 0.000, 1)
```

stand for

```
Call seqname("Action Set") .at
(time, "script", loop, interval,
tiebreak, drop threshold)
```

Sequence Naming

The sequence can be given any name you want. It's a good idea to keep the word "seq" somewhere in the name so that you know it's a sequence.

Action Sets

Sequences that are grouped together are called Action Sets. Each sequencing object (which we named **seq**) can have multiple Action Sets. Action Sets are individual timelines that run independently, which allows you to stop or pause one while the others continue to run. In Listing 10-2, we have only one Action

Set named **1**. (We'll use the words "Action Set" and "timeline" interchangeably from this point.) To create another timeline, simply substitute another number or word where the **1** is in the Action Set. You must remember that this timeline must now be started and stopped independently. For performance reasons, you should place multiple Action Sets on one sequencing object rather than individual Action Sets on multiple sequencing objects.

At Method

The At method tells the function "at" what time to trigger. Time is measured in terms of elapsed time since the Action Set began playing. In Listing 10-2, the Action Set started with the following command:

```
Sub Window_onload()
Call Seq("1").Play
```

This command caused the Action Set 1 to start playing when all pictures and text had finished loading on the screen. Time is measured in the format **_seconds.milliseconds_**. Because the timing is based on the computer's internal clock, actions will be triggered at the same time on all computers regardless of the machine's speed.

Those numbers act as the controls for the following parameters:

Loop: The loop is set to 1 in our example. In other words, it plays only once. If the number is set higher, the program will loop more times. (Set at 5, for example, the program will loop 5 times.) If it is set to −1, the program will loop forever.

Interval: In our example, the interval is set to 0.000. This parameter controls how often the loop is executed. The fastest that the loop can be executed is 0.020, or every 20 milliseconds. The default is 0.033 (33 milliseconds), which means that the loop will happen 30 times per second.

Tiebreaker: The tiebreaker controls what happens if two functions are set to trigger at the same time. In Listing 10-2, it is set to 1. The priority of an action decreases as the number becomes larger. The most important action has a value of 0. The least important value that can be given is −1.

Drop Threshold: We left one value out of our string. This optional parameter is used when many events are being executed at the same time. Imagine that you triggered 5 animations at 5 seconds into the sequence. On a slow computer, these animations may be able to execute only one at a time. It is conceivable that an event may not be triggered until seconds after it was supposed to execute. In a time-critical sequence, you may not wish this event to trigger at all if it will be late. The drop threshold tells the computer that if the event has not triggered by, for example, 5 seconds after it should have, then it shouldn't occur at all. This specification helps to stage choreography of the presentation. The default value is −1, which means that the event should always be triggered no matter how late it is.

Controlling the Sequence

So far we've learned how to start a sequence when the script loads and how to add additional Action Sets or timelines. What if we want to start an action set when a button is clicked or we want to pause the sequence or stop it all together? Table 10-1 lists some options.

TABLE 10-1. METHODS FOR CONTROLLING THE SEQUENCE

Method	Description	Parameters
Play	Starts the Action Set.	None
Pause	Pauses play of an Action Set. Stops playback time at its current value. Play method will restart the timeline.	None
Stop	Stops play of an Action Set. Playback time is set to 0.	None
Seek	Jumps around in the Action Set. Set time to the position to which to jump.	Time

Play example: **Seq ("2").play()**

We've seen how to play an Action Set when the page loads. Now we will see how to trigger one after the page is loaded.

You may remember that after 1 second the **pic1_show** function was executed by the timeline. If we had another Action Set created, we could have executed this second function. Imagine that we have a second Action Set called **Seq ("2")**. If we wanted to trigger it after the **pic1** graphic was made visible, we would have added the following statement to the **pic1_show** function:

```
Sub pic1_show()

pic1.filters(0).apply()
pic1.style.visibility = "visible"
pic1.filters(0).play()
Seq ("2").play()

End Sub
```

We now have a series of animations that happen in sequence. The content depends on the fact that one animation finishes before the next one starts. On a slower machine, however, the second animation starts before the first one finishes — ruining the content. One way to work around this performance issue is to have the second animation play only when the first one finishes.

Pause example: **Seq ("2").pause()**

Pausing an Action Set freezes the time at the moment when it is paused. Thus, if you pause an Action Set at 3 seconds and don't restart it until 5 seconds later, the time for that Action Set is still set at 3 seconds, not 8 seconds. If a user must sit through a slideshow presentation that last more than a few minutes, it is nice to include a pause button that allows the user to control the playback of the slideshow. This example illustrates how the author's thinking must change when dealing with the stage- versus page-based metaphors for web authoring.

TIP
......

As noted earlier, all computers don't play back the same functions at the same speed. That's why the drop threshold value was implemented.

Stop example: **Seq ("2").stop()**

This method stops the playback of the action set permanently and resets the time to 0. If a play command is then issued for this function, the Action Set plays back from the beginning.

Seek example: **Seq ("2").seek()**

Seeking is similar to the jumping around in the Score in Macromedia Director. It allows you to reuse functions. In the example given above, if the Action Set was triggered it would jump to the 8 seconds mark on Action Set 1. At 8 seconds on Action Set 1, the **pic3_show** function is triggered. The seek method, therefore, changes the amount of elapsed time that is stored in the time parameter.

SUMMARY

The Sequence control is the master script for developing stage-based presentations of web content. The JavaScript example described in this chapter is a universal script that will allow you to trigger actions over time. It works in both Netscape 4.0 and Internet Explorer 4.0. It is also useful as a basis for cross-platform development. When combined with the **IF THEN** structures (discussed in Chapter 1), it allows you to make almost any presentation compatible across a variety of platforms.

The Active X/VBScript example is just as powerful and easier to use. It is, however, proprietary to Internet Explorer 4 for PC; it will not work with the Macintosh or UNIX flavors of Internet Explorer 4. In addition to the functionality available with the JavaScript timeline, it brings the ability to stop, pause, and seek in the timeline. These powerful features allow for the reuse of bits of code and for better interactivity. They come at the great cost of compatibility, unfortunately.

LINKS

Microsoft Multimedia Controls (Sequencer)
http://www.microsoft.com/directx/dxm/help/da/DA_E0021.htm

INTERNET EXPLORER 4'S MULTIMEDIA CONTROLS

BACKGROUND

Standards committees like W3C are inhibited by one small detail: They need to get the standard right the first time. As a result, they are not free to experiment with technologies and they can't harness platform-specific strengths. A company like Microsoft, however, suffers from no such limitations. Its entire business is built on putting out products and then making incremental improvements. It can therefore write platform-specific code and tie Windows into everything it creates. Both Netscape and Microsoft have been guilty of this approach in the past. If both companies implemented only W3C standards, then we would still be working out the syntax for tables.

Microsoft has chosen to extend the capabilities of the Internet Explorer 4 browser without following any other group's standards. If developers find these capabilities useful, then perhaps W3C will eventually create a standard for them.

UNDERLYING TECHNOLOGY

What are **Active X multimedia controls** and what do they look like? As a developer you will interact with them through HTML-

173

like parameter tags. If you have passed parameters to a Java applet, then the multimedia controls look much the same. If you are using the Path Control, for example, you will designate the points between which the object (any **DIV** tag) will travel and specify how long it will take.

Compatibility is the main issue with Active X controls. These controls work only in Internet Explorer 4+ on Windows 95/98 and NT machines. They do not work with Windows 3.1 because of limits in the 16-bit operating system. They are also incompatible with the Sun and Macintosh Internet Explorer 4.0 implementations. Consequently, these controls should be used sparingly. If you work in a closed, Windows-only environment, such as a corporate intranet, and are developing an Internet Explorer 4+ Active Channel, then using these controls makes sense. They are easy to configure by using parameters within HTML, and they are built into the operating system to avoid lengthy downloads.

At this point, you might say, "OK, so this technology is totally incompatible and runs only in Windows; why is he writing about it?" In fact, these controls provide some very cool multimedia functionality. As mentioned earlier, I spent a few years developing CD-ROMs, mostly in Macromedia Authorware and Director. When I moved over to web development, I felt very inhibited by the media. Worrying about download times and writing HTML for static web pages was a major change from CD-ROM, which offered a blazingly fast (by comparison) 150KB/s transfer rate for 1× CD-ROM. Shockwave, however, allowed me to leverage my previous skills to the web. Nevertheless, Shockwave is still confined to a box on the screen and can't interact with the rest of the screen.

The multimedia controls will be very familiar to Director and Authorware developers. They bring some of the functionality of these programs to the web with smaller downloads and greater freedom to interact with and control all objects on the screen.

Thus, the Active X multimedia controls are very efficient. They run very well on any Pentium machine. Because they are built into Internet Explorer 4+, they don't need to be down-loaded, unlike other Active X controls. This setup also makes them incompatible with Netscape. In contrast, Windows-based Netscape users can use a plug-in such as nCompass to view down-loadable Active X controls. This option won't work with the multimedia controls.

EXAMPLES

Many Active X controls are built into Internet Explorer 4. Here, we'll concentrate on four controls that make multimedia easier, known collectively as the Direct Animation multimedia controls. The four are the Sequencer control, Sprite controls, Structure Graphics control, and Path control. Because these controls are built into Internet Explorer 4, they don't need to be downloaded.

The Sequencer Control

For Macromedia Director users, the **Sequencer control** will bring back memories of the Score feature. This control allows you to make events occur over time, an essential element of on-line storytelling. The Sequencer control allows you to trigger functions at specific times. By combining many actions under this control, you can create much more complex actions. JavaScript allows you to write a similar control using the setTimeout method, though this task is much more difficult. It is also possible to write a script in JavaScript that provides all the functionality of this control and is cross-browser compatible. One such JavaScript example appears in Chapter 10.

Now let's take a look at the Sequencer control.* In your program, you must first call the Active X control. Normally you would specify a URL from which the Active X component should be downloaded. Because these components are built into

---

*For a real-world example of this control, subscribe to the active desktop component at Discovery Channel Online and look at the feature stories.

Internet Explorer 4, however, you just need the following line:

```
<OBJECT ID="Seq"CLASSID="CLSID:
B0A6BAE2-AAF0-11d0-A152-
00A0C908DB96"></OBJECT>
```

This command loads the component into memory. Notice in the code that the Sequencer component is started when the page is fully loaded. Its initiation is carried out with the following function. (Although we are using VBScript for this example, this task can also be done with JavaScript.)

```
Sub Window_onload()
Call Seq("1").Play
End Sub
```

This function starts the Sequencer control when the page is fully loaded. Now we can trigger any function whenever we like.

```
Sub Seq_OnInit()
Call seq("1").at(1.000, "pic1_show", 1, 0.000, 1)
Call seq("1").at(3.000, "pic2_show", 1, 0.000, 1)
Call seq("1").at(6.000, "pic1_hide", 1, 0.000, 1)
Call seq("1").at(8.000, "pic3_show", 1, 0.000, 1)
Call seq("1").at(10.200, "pic2_hide", 1, 0.000, 1)
Call seq("1").at(11.100, "pic3_hide", 1, 0.000, 1)
End Sub
```

Let's look at what the first line in the sequence means:

```
Call seq("1").at(1.000, "pic1_show", 1, 0.000, 1)
```

Those numbers stand for

```
Call seqname("Action Set") .at (time, "script", loop,
interval, tiebreak)
```

Thus this line would read: Start the **seq** sequence 1 second after the page loads and trigger the **pic1_show** function so that it plays once with no looping.

Very easy. If you want to trigger other functions at different times, just change the time and the function name. Our example shows and hides pictures—a helpful operation for slideshows or for storytelling.

Notice that the loop is set to 1 in our example. That means the script plays only once. To make it play five times, increase the number to 5. To make it play an infinite number of times, make the number −1.

The interval controls how long the script should wait between loops. In our example, it is set to 0.000. The fastest the loop can be executed is 0.020, which is every 20 milliseconds. The default is 0.033 (33 milliseconds), which is 30 times per second.

The tiebreaker controls the outcome if two functions are set to begin at the same time. In our example, it is set to 1. The priority of an action decreases as the number becomes larger. The most important action has a value of 0. The least important value that can be given is −1.

The Sequencer control is a powerful aid for creating time-based presentations and storytelling. This control allows the creation of web pages that act more like CD-ROM-based multimedia than traditional web pages.

The Sprite Control

The **Sprite control** is basically an upgrade to animated GIF images. It does have some extra advantages, however. First, it is scriptable. You can have one type of animation that occurs on mouseover, another that appears when the user clicks an element, and a third that runs when the mouse isn't near the image. Second, the graphic file is stored as one big strip of graphics, much like a filmstrip. This setup makes it easy for a graphic artist to change the file without running it through a GIF animation program again. Frames can be reused, and the play rate can be controlled from HTML without having to recompile the animated GIF.

Let's look at the code.

```
<OBJECT ID="Robot1" STYLE="position:
absolute; left:10;
top:10; WIDTH:73; HEIGHT:73; z-index:1;
visibility: visible; cursor:hand" CLASSID =
"clsid:FD179533-D86E-11d0-89D6-00A0C90833E6">
<PARAM NAME="Repeat" VALUE="-1">
<PARAM NAME="PlayRate" VALUE="9">
<PARAM NAME="NumFrames" VALUE="4">
<PARAM NAME="NumFramesAcross" VALUE="1">
<PARAM NAME="NumFramesDown" VALUE="4">
<PARAM NAME="SourceURL"
VALUE="http://www.ruleweb.com/dhtml/
activexanimate/graphics/ani_bots.gif">
<PARAM NAME="MouseEventsEnabled"
VALUE="True">
<PARAM NAME="AutoStart" VALUE="1">
<PARAM NAME="UseColorKey" VALUE="1">
<PARAM NAME="ColorKey"
VALUE="255,255,255">
<PARAM NAME="FrameMap"
VALUE="1,1;2,1;1,1;3,1;4,1">
</OBJECT>
```

In the first line, we load the Active X component and specify its location in a manner similar to placing style sheets.

The **Repeat** value is set to −1 for an infinitely repeating loop. You may also set any number you like.

The **PlayRate** parameter determines how fast the animation will play. You may need to experiment with this value to get the right speed.

NumFrames is the total number of frames that make up the filmstrip. The filmstrip can also be multiple frames down, so that a four-frame filmstrip might really take the form of a two-by-two block. (I like to keep the graphics in a single strip.)

The **SourceURL** parameter indicates where the filmstrip graphic is found.

MouseEventsEnabled is set to true, which allows you to have the graphic change on mouse events.

AutoStart makes the animation play when the graphic is loaded. You can also choose to have the animation start on a mouse event.

The **UseColorKey** and **ColorKey** variables are used to make a color in the graphic transparent.

The **FrameMap** parameter determines the order in which the frames play. The frames are determined by two numbers (column number, row number) separated by a semicolon. Frames can be reused multiple times, which saves download time.

Although the Sprite Active X component does improve on the animated GIF standard, it doesn't provide enough incentives to switch to this proprietary technology. You might want to stick with animated GIF images unless you know your web page will be viewed only in Internet Explorer 4.

The Structured Graphics Control

The **Structured Graphics control** should really be called the Vector Graphics control. It allows Internet Explorer 4 pages to display vector graphics. There are two kinds of graphics: raster graphics and vector graphics. Raster graphics are types like GIF, JPG, and PICT; they are one size only and can't be scaled without noticeable blurring and artifacts. Vector graphics are produced by programs like Macromedia Freehand and Flash; they can be scaled without losing clarity. Vector graphics are much smaller in terms of download size than are raster graphics. That's why Flash downloads are much faster than downloads of Director-based Shockwave.

This control, in its current form, doesn't live up to its full potential. Although the web is begging for a vector graphics standard, certain elements of this control make it very difficult to work with. It is hard to position, slow to draw to the screen once loaded, and sometimes doesn't draw at all. This unreliability is clearly a problem.

Despite these drawbacks, this control does offer some nice features. These graphics can be controlled and manipulated by scripting. In addition to smooth resizing, they can be rotated in all three dimensions. Their download size is very small and is contained in a text file that can be stored in HTML or in an external file. The file is created by converting a Windows Metafile (WMF) into a text file. Windows Metafiles can be exported from Freehand. The conversion program (from WMF to text file) is part of the Microsoft Internet SDK.

The vector image is called and positioned with the following Active X control:

```
<OBJECT id=SG1 STYLE="POSITION:ABSOLUTE;
HEIGHT: 300; LEFT: -50; TOP: -50;
WIDTH: 300; ZINDEX: 0" CLASSID =
"CLSID:369303C2-D7AC-11D0-89D5-00A0C90833E6">
```

The lines of numbers in the **<PARAM>** are the coordinates generated by the conversion program from the Internet SDK. You don't have to enter the coordinates.

The rotations in the x, y, and z axes are controlled by the script at the top. Initially the graphic is drawn and scaled to 50% of its original size, and the rotation is then started. This rotation is controlled by the following lines:

```
Sub Window_OnLoad()
call SG1.Scale(0.50, 0.50, 0.50)
RotateAll
end sub
```

The rate at which it rotates is controlled by the following lines:

```
Sub RotateAll
Call SG1.Rotate(0,0,-10)
```

```
FILK = Window.SetTimeOut("Call
RotateAll", 10, "VBScript")
End Sub
```

The −10 in the second line controls the degree of rotation in the clockwise axis. The first two numbers—the horizontal and vertical axes—are set to zero so that no rotation happens along those axes. Try experimenting with these numbers.

Despite its limitations, the Structured Graphics control can create large-scale images on the web with very small downloads. It also provides rotation in three dimensions. One favorite trick is to have a vector image rotate or fly into position and then fade into a JPG or GIF image. This effect combines the flexibility of vector with the photorealistic aspects of raster images.

The Path Control

The Path control allows for objects to be animated along paths. It may seem redundant at first. One of the strengths of Dynamic HTML is its ability to move objects around the screen. In fact, path animation is one of the few features that works equally well in both Netscape 4 and Internet Explorer 4.

So why reinvent the wheel? The Path control makes it very easy to create simple animations or complex animations. The code to create animation in Dynamic HTML can be fairly complicated and doesn't lend itself to beginners. The Path control is simple and can easily be set up by someone who knows only HTML.

Let's look at the code. First, the Active X component must be loaded:

```
<OBJECT ID="robotPath" CLASSID =
"CLSID:D7A7D7C3-D47F-11D0-89D3-
00A0C90833E6">
```

Next, the Path control must be told to run as soon as the entire page has loaded. It is important to wait for the page to load; otherwise the control may animate the graphic too soon. Nothing looks worse than a broken graphic icon animating across the screen. This timing is handled with the onload event in the body tag and triggers the following function:

```
robotPath.play();
```

The graphic then begins animating along the path. The graphic that will be animated must be given a name (in this case, **robot**), so that the control knows which graphic to use.

Now let's look at the control.

```
<PARAM NAME="AutoStart" VALUE="0">
<PARAM NAME="Bounce" VALUE="0">
<PARAM NAME="Duration" VALUE="2.0">
<PARAM NAME="Repeat" VALUE="1">
<PARAM NAME="Shape"
VALUE="PolyLine(2, 0,150, 350,150)">
<PARAM NAME="Target" VALUE="robot">
</OBJECT>
```

This script is very easy to understand. The **AutoStart** parameter is self-explanatory. If it is 1, then the script autostarts; if it is 0, then it does not. **Bounce** makes the animation go back and forth along its path. **Duration** determines the time from the start of the path until it reaches the end. **Repeat** makes the path play a certain number of times. Entering -1 here will make the loop repeat infinitely. It can give a great effect when combined with **Bounce**.

Four shapes of the path are possible:

- Polyline: The polyline is a set of straight paths. It can be one straight line or a series of straight lines.
- Spline: The spline follows a series of coordinates that are smoothed using a spline-based path. This method produces smooth, complex paths. In the following example, the first number tells the number of points on the path

and the rest of the numbers are (x, y) coordinates for the 12 points on the path:

```
<PARAM NAME="Shape" VALUE="spline
(12,20,50, 30,30, 50,10, 80,40, 110,60,
130,50, 140,30, 130,10, 110,20, 80,40,
50,60, 20,50)">
```

- Rectangle
- Polygon

Rectangles and polygons are seldom used. As you can see, the Path control is great for producing quick animations in Internet Explorer 4-only pages. All you need is the set of coordinates that the animation will follow, and you're ready to go. The spline-based path is especially time-saving, as it also provides smoothing. All in all, the Path control is a powerful addition to the animation capabilities that already exist in Internet Explorer 4.

SUMMARY

The Active X multimedia controls are powerful stuff. Microsoft has leveraged some of the features of its operating system to provide web developers with tools that are both easy to use and unique to web development. In using them, however, we lose the ability to serve Netscape users and all Internet Explorer users on other platforms besides Windows. We can only hope that Netscape or W3C will accept these easy-to-use tools as a challenge and will create some standards-based tools with similar functionality. Until then, brush up on your browser detection techniques (see Chapter 1) and be ready to create multiple pages. Once you see the capabilities of these tools, you may have a hard time returning to animated GIF images to create multimedia.

LINKS

Active X Multimedia Controls
http://www.microsoft.com/directx/dxm/help/da/DA_E0019.htm

Windows MetaFile-to-Structured-Graphics Converter

http://www.microsoft.com/directx/dxm/help/da/da_e0025.htm

Active X Sequencer Control Example

http://www.ruleweb.com/dhtml/Sequence/jeffsequencex.html

Sprite Control Example

http://www.ruleweb.com/dhtml/activeexanimate/index.html

Structured Graphics Control Examples

http://www.ruleweb.com/dhtml/vector/vectorx.html and
http://www.ruleweb.com/dhtml/flyin/flyin.html

Path Control Example

http://www.ruleweb.com/dhtml/path_control/path_code.html

FONTS

BACKGROUND

Fonts have been a long-neglected area of web page development.

In 1984, the first laser printers for the Macintosh were introduced. I had an Apple IIe at the time and was jealous (of everything except the lack of games, that is). The Macintosh had always enjoyed good font support, but the results were poor when documents were printed out on a dot matrix printer. The Laserwriter system changed all that. Suddenly the printouts looked better than what was appearing on the screen. PostScript, the technology behind laser printers, changed everything. The desktop publishing revolution was on.

The World Wide Web has spurred a similar revolution in publishing. You can tell that the Internet and World Wide Web were both built by engineers, however, because of the lag in developing a method to display fonts on the web. It took a push by designers to turn downloadable web fonts into a reality. In the past, designers had to make do with the limited number of system fonts that ship on PCs and Macintosh computers. Even when common fonts exist, the cross-platform fonts are inevitably rendered smaller on the Macintosh, even if the point size is the same. When it is important that a font have an attractive appearance, designers often create a graphic of the font to ensure that it will look the same on all browsers in JPG or GIF format.

Security has been another problem for web fonts. Some people have spent their entire lives developing fonts in such programs as Macromedia Fontographer. A few of the fonts may become very popular, while others are destined for obscurity. Fonts are licensed by the manufacturer to graphic designers. Some of these fonts can be surprisingly expensive, and their developers must protect their investment from getting "loose" on the web where others can use the fonts without paying royalties. Both Microsoft and Netscape have taken steps to address this concern in their version 4.0 browsers. W3C is also working on a standard that should satisfy all parties. Currently, both Microsoft and Netscape browsers encode each font so that it can be downloaded from only one server. Any attempts to steal the font and install it on another server won't work.

Even though Microsoft and Netscape have different standards for their version 4.0 browsers, the processes by which you create downloadable fonts for these browsers are very similar.

> **TIP**
> ......
> Fonts often render smaller on the Macintosh.

UNDERLYING TECHNOLOGY

As with most things in the version 4.0 browsers, a similar, but different, method is used for encoding fonts.

Netscape uses a technology from Bitstream called TrueDoc. When built into authoring tools and web browsers, TrueDoc provides for the secure transfer of font data from the web author's server to the web viewer's system. We'll talk more about TrueDoc in the section on Netscape font encoding.

Microsoft's font embedding is based on TrueType fonts. These fonts are the same ones that you use on your PC or Macintosh computer.

NETSCAPE

Fonts are displayed in Netscape 4.01 and higher via a built-in program called **Character Shape Player (CSP)**. Interestingly,

Netscape 4.0 itself does not include this technology. Instead, CSP is a rendering engine that interprets the downloaded fonts and makes them available to the browser. Downloadable fonts are contained in a file called a **font definition file** [also called a **Portable Font Resource (PFR)** file for short]. As we will discuss later, the font can be designated in HTML by using CSS or the **<FONT>** tag.

PFR files are much smaller than the actual font files that you load into an operating system. A TrueType I font can be as large as 48K in its operating system form. When it is converted to a PFR format, it takes up less than 15K. Although 15K is still fairly large, it is small enough to download over a 28.8 modem or higher with very little waiting time. PFR files are also stored in the browser cache so that they can be reused without being downloaded yet again.

Creating the PFR File

Creating the PFR file is fairly easy, but still takes some preparation. The author must have the desired font installed on his or her machine in TrueType or PostScript format. The page must be created in an authoring tool that includes the CSR. HexWeb Typograph 2.0 from HexMac is a good example of such a tool (Figure 12-1). The authoring tool converts the font from the author's machine into a PFR file that then must be put on the server.

While you are encoding the PFR file, you will be asked the domain name of the server that should hold the file. This step is a security measure to ensure that no one steals the font files. Any

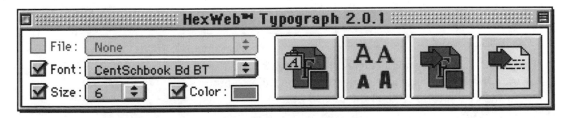

FIGURE 12-1. HexWeb Typograph 2.0.1 web font tool for Netscape 4

attempt to download the PFR file from a different domain will abort the font download.

PFR files can contain definitions for more than one font. Thus, if you are using several different fonts on a page, there is no need to create multiple PFR files.

Also, to save downloading time, some authoring programs will allow you to encode only the specific letters that you are using on your page. Say that you had "Discovery Channel" in a special font. The program would only encode the letters "D-I-S-C-O-V-E-R-Y-H-A-N-L." This option saves a great deal of time when downloading (Figure 12-2).

Preparing the Server

The PFR is a new file type, so the server must be made aware of it before it can communicate properly with the browser. You must change the settings on the server to accept the

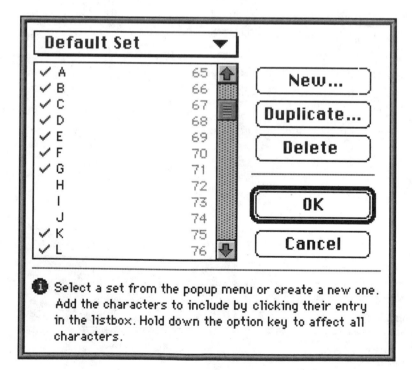

FIGURE 12-2.
Letter-by-letter encoding in HexWeb Typograph 2.0.1

`application/font-tdpfr` MIME type and the `.pfr` file extension.

Formatting Style Sheets and the `<FONT>` Tag

Netscape is smart when it comes to displaying fonts. If the user already has a font installed on his or her machine, then Netscape will use this font from the user's hard drive to display it. If the font is not present, Netscape will download the font so that it can display correctly.

Netscape needs to know where the external PFR file is located. The author must therefore include a **`<LINK>`** tag in the **`<HEAD>`** of the HTML file. The full code looks like this:

```
<LINK REL="fontdef"
SRC="fonts/jeffsfont.pfr">
```

If more than one PFR file is being used in the page, you must use multiple **`<LINK>`** tags to connect them.

One way to define the font is with the traditional **`<FONT>`** tag. Using the **FACE** attribute, you can set up several fonts from which the browser can choose. The first one in the list should be the downloadable font. The other fonts in the list should be commonly used or system fonts that employ similar spacing to your downloadable font. If something goes wrong with the download or if the browser is not compatible (as is the case with Internet Explorer), then the browser will use these backup fonts. Here's an example of a font definition:

```
<FONT FACE="Fleetwood,
Arial, serif">...</FONT>
```

Note that you need to use the "real name" of the font here, *not* the name you gave to the PFR file.

Formatting with Cascading Style Sheets

CSS uses the font-family attribute. Chapter 3 discusses this issue in more depth, but here's a quick example of how to designate a font using style sheets:

```
<STYLE TYPE="text/css">
#Text {
font-family: Fleetwood, Arial, serif;
font-size: 24pt;
color: #FFFFFF;
}
</STYLE>
```

Notes on Netscape 4's Font Handling

In general, Netscape has provided a neat way to create download-able fonts. Nevertheless, its system has at least two problems.

First, Netscape does not provide a free tool that allows you to encode PFR files. In fact, several popular tools, such as NetObjects Fusion and Allaire Homesite, lack PFR encoding software. One of the few tools with this capability is HexWeb Typograph 2.0. Interestingly, HexWeb has developed an Active X plug-in that allows Internet Explorer 4 users to view fonts created in PFR files. Details are available at http://www.truedoc.com/webpages/intro/howto_ie.htm.

Second, Netscape may display the page before the PFR file has been downloaded. A screen redraw must then occur after the PFR finishes downloading. That is, the screen gives a jerk and then redraws. This transition is very abrupt and reminds us why many people do not consider the web to be a mature medium like television. Can you imagine text on TV reformatting sponta-neously in the middle of Dan Rather's "News Brief"? If the web is to become a mature medium, then such problems must be resolved.

INTERNET EXPLORER

Microsoft follows much the same pattern as Netscape does for encoding fonts for download. First, fonts must be prepared using a program called **Web Embedding Fonts Tool (WEFT)**, illus-trated in Figure 12-3.

The tool processes the fonts on the author's machine and makes them ready for downloading. Fonts are encoded in an

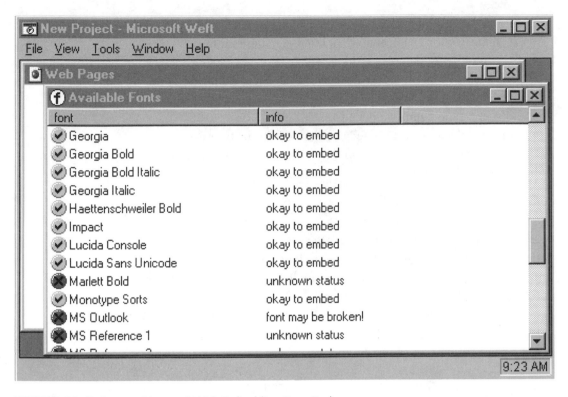

FIGURE 12-3. Fonts in Microsoft Web Embedding Fonts Tool

Embeddable Open Type (EOT) file. Not all fonts can be prepared for downloading, however. Only TrueType fonts can be encoded.

Before you begin working with a font, you must check the permissions associated with it. There are several levels of permissions.

- *No-embedding* permissions are rarely used. Fonts with this type of permission cannot be included in your web pages because the creator has chosen not to allow them to be used by other authors. Sometimes these fonts are demonstration fonts that can be upgraded to embeddable fonts by contacting the creator.
- *Print and preview* fonts can be embedded, but only in static web pages (that is, pages that load and are not

changed after loading). If the page includes user interaction or manipulation of the fonts, these fonts cannot be used.

- *Editable* fonts can be embedded after they are prepared in a tool such as WEFT. These fonts can be fully manipulated and embedded.
- *Installable* fonts are treated as editable fonts by Internet Explorer 4.0. Despite their name, they are not installed in the user's fonts folder.

The size of downloadable fonts is even smaller in Internet Explorer 4 than in Netscape 4. In Netscape, certain precautions must be taken to ensure that only the letters you need are encoded. Normally, Netscape will encode all letters in a certain font. Microsoft's WEFT, on the other hand, looks at the page after you have created it and analyzes the fonts, picking only the letters you used to be encoded. This tactic significantly reduces the size of download. Table 12-1 provides some examples of downloadable fonts for Internet Explorer 4.

TABLE 12-1. SELECTED DOWNLOADABLE FONTS FOR INTERNET EXPLORER 4

Font	Characters in the Font	Size (K)
French Script MT	52	11.1K
Copyblot	2	4.23K
Dingblots (page 1)	3	2.56K

WEFT: The Encoding Tool

Microsoft is famous for giving tools away. The WEFT encoding tool can be downloaded for free from http://www.microsoft.com/typography/web/embedding/weft/. In the steps below, we explain some of the most important tasks that you can undertake with WEFT.

1. **Analyzing Fonts**
   Open WEFT. Choose View: Available Fonts to see a complete list of fonts that can be encoded by WEFT and used on a web

page. A check mark means that the font can be embedded, a question mark means that it is a core font of all Windows systems and does not need to be embedded, and an "X" means that it is not embeddable.

2. **Placing Fonts on Your Page**
   Fonts can be placed on the page using the same methods described earlier in the "Netscape" section. Use either the `<FONT>` tag or CSS. Because WEFT uses Internet Explorer to analyze the pages, it is a good idea to preview your work in this browser.

3. **Running WEFT**
   A. The WEFT wizard will start automatically when you run WEFT. By following the steps in the wizard, you can encode the page you have just finished. It is important that the page be completed before you encode.
   B. *Internet Access:* You can designate a "work" directory on your local drive where the encoded fonts will be copied or you can give an FTP address of your web server and have the files copied there.
   C. *Page List:* Enter the name of the page you wish to encode. You should enter the entire path to the page, such as http://www.discovery.com/online.html or file:///c:/weft/test.htm. The file can be encoded either on the local drive or on the server.
   D. Once you have decided which pages to analyze, press the "Analyze pages!" button at the bottom right of the screen.
   E. Once the page has been analyzed, the font usage screen will appear. Here you can remove and edit the fonts that will be encoded. This page also reports how many characters of each font will be encoded.
   F. *Creating and Posting the Font Objects:* Here you enter the path to your FTP server or the location on your hard drive where the font objects will reside.
   G. *Publishing:* At this point, WEFT copies *modified* copies of your HTML back to the folder. You should make backups of your HTML before undertaking this step. WEFT adds

code that includes information on the location of the EOT
files containing the encoded fonts.

H. *Dynamic Content:* Microsoft has warned that Dynamic
HTML may cause problems in the encoding process, especially if you use scripting to modify fonts. If you'll be creating cutting-edge pages with 3-D rotating text (or even
slightly less complicated pages), check your code and make
backups before publishing.

I. *Saving Information:* You can save a WEFT project to be
modified later.

Other Issues

Internet Explorer's security features will trigger a warning when
the EOT files are being downloaded. This warning is generated
at the default security level.

Unlike Netscape 4, Internet Explorer 4 downloads the
EOT files before it renders the fonts to the screen. This approach
avoids the "flash" seen in Netscape when it switches to the downloaded font.

COMPATIBILITY BETWEEN NETSCAPE 4 AND INTERNET EXPLORER 4

Where do these font management schemes leave us on the cross-
platform compatibility question? Despite total incompatibility
of the two font formats, there is hope. Both standards use the
<FONT> tag and CSS to specify the font types that are used, so at
least part of the process is compatible.

Netscape uses the **<LINK>** tag to embed its PFR files, as in
the following example:

```
<LINK REL="fontdef"
SRC="fonts/jeffsfont.pfr">
```

Because Microsoft doesn't recognize the **<LINK>** tag, it will
ignore this command. Netscape, on the other hand, will use it to
download the correct PFR file.

Microsoft will use the code inserted by the WEFT into the Cascading Style Sheet. This code will look similar to the following example:

```
@font face {font family: Goudy Stout;
font-style: normal; font-weight: 700;
src: url(GOUDYSTO.eot);}
```

This code will be ignored by Netscape.

Thus, because the browsers will ignore the font source files of the other browsers, compatibility exists. Although this approach does require encoding the same fonts once for each browser, in the end there is compatibility without having to write lots of **IF THEN** statements or use browser detects.

W3C Standards

W3C is currently working on a standard for web font downloading. It is trying to ensure that web authors have access to a diverse set of fonts in many languages. It has set forth a list of objectives for this standard (the following are taken from the W3C web site, http://www.w3.org/fonts/):

- A suitable font format that provides support for kerning, ligatures, and resolution independency.
- Specification and decoding software that is freely available.
- A mechanism whereby fonts can be downloaded on request over the web and, if necessary, converted to the format required by a particular platform's addressing, naming, and matching scheme for font resources.
- A supply of fonts.

No official specifications have been released on downloadable fonts, but developers can post their feedback on web fonts on a W3C-sponsored forum.

SUMMARY

It is surprising that a standard for web fonts has taken so long to make it to the web. This frontier remains the last area over which designers have little control. Once a standard is established and CSS is firmly entrenched, then designers should gain the same level of control that they have enjoyed in programs such as Adobe Pagemaker.

At this point, the Microsoft method has greater support than the Netscape method. Netscape's lack of a free encoding tool has also hampered acceptance of its web font management system. Currently, Microsoft's implementation is closer to the standard envisioned by W3C.

LINKS

Netscape

http://www.hexmac.com

http://www.hexmac.com/hexmac/engl/webtools/typograph2/
	typograph2.html

http://developer.netscape.com/news/viewsource/
	goodman_fonts.html

http://www.bitstream.com/world/

Internet Explorer

http://www.microsoft.com/msdn/sdk/inetsdk/help/dhtml/
	content/font_embed.htm

http://www.microsoft.com/typography/default.htm

http://www.microsoft.com/typography/web/embedding/weft/

W3C

http://www.w3c.org/fonts/

CREATING CHANNELS

BACKGROUND

Evolution of Push Technology

First came the bookmark list. You could mark your favorite web pages and return to check them whenever you wanted. You had to guess when new content was put up, and sometimes you might forget about a site for months at a time, but you received the information often enough.

Mailing lists were the first true **push technology**. These newsletters, such as DevEdge from Netscape or Adam Engst's Macintosh newsletter TidBITS, came through every few weeks. Sometimes you might read them, and sometimes they went directly into the trash.

Then came push technology with Pointcast Networks at its forefront. I installed a very early version of Pointcast, and it held my technical fascination for several weeks—before it became annoying, that is, and I uninstalled it. By this time, however, the genie was out of the bottle. Content providers on the web envisioned pushing their own customized newsletters to millions of ravenous consumers on the web. Customers dreamed about being delivered just what they needed, when they needed it.

This technology has some problems, however. Pointcast, for example, may update its customers every hour or so with the latest news. By some estimates, Pointcast can account for as much as 10% of Internet traffic at certain times of the day (usually on the hour). Microsoft and Netscape thought that this concept was a great idea and soon climbed aboard the bandwagon.

Channel-Based Push Technology

Push technology, in the form of channels, has clearly arrived. A **channel** is a set of web pages that use push technology to deliver their content automatically to the user's computer in a predetermined manner, rather than being pulled in by an explicit user interaction. Users can customize what, when, and how often channel information is pushed to their desktops. Rich, dynamic, interactive content, based on HTML and JavaScript, can be automatically sent to the desktop and viewed in either a browser window or full-screen mode.

Riding on a wave of hype about television's convergence with the PC, channels have entered the mainstream of web development. Channels are inherently no different than web pages. What is different is the way that they are delivered. With regular web pages, the user must enter the URL or go to a bookmark or a favorite list. With push technology, the information is delivered to the user's computer's hard drive on a regularly scheduled basis, usually in the middle of the night when the user is away from the machine. This automatic delivery system saves the consumer the headache of downloading large pages from the web.

Both Microsoft and Netscape have been touting channels as a significantly different technology; in fact, they are not. Channels, just like normal web pages, are authored using HTML, JavaScript, VBScript, and Dynamic HTML. A page can act as both a channel and a web page. At Discovery, for example, we provide an alternative channel for Internet Explorer 4 users. This channel replicates our home page, but adds a number of Dynamic HTML elements. Because this page is seen only by our Internet Explorer 4 viewers, we can use the newest browser technologies to make the page interesting and dynamic. Indeed, one nice thing about push channels in general is that you can use the newest browser technologies because you need not worry about backward browser compatibility. The older browsers will never see this content unless you decide to send it to them.

Channels can incorporate any kind of content you'd normally place on a web site, and you can turn a web site into a channel with only a few lines of JavaScript code. You'll probably want to include larger, more complex files that bring your channel to life, though, simply because normal bandwidth considerations aren't as much of a concern with push technology as they are with traditional web downloading.

Channels are supposed to deliver high-bandwidth, personalized information to the desktop with no download time. In reality, they often deliver bandwidth-hogging material that is almost never read by the consumer. Despite Microsoft and Netscape's hopes, most content providers have simply repackaged their existing materials for channels. They have not created the immersive multimedia experiences that channels are capable of providing.

NETSCAPE CHANNELS

Netcaster

Netcaster is the "receiver" for channels that are built into Netscape 4.01 and later releases. It was launched shortly after Communicator 4.0 shipped and was in beta testing at the time of Communicator's original release.

Netcaster and Microsoft's channel bar are very similar in appearance and function. Netcaster pops out from the right side of the screen, presenting the user with buttons for Netcaster "channels" (Figure 13-1). Netcaster ships with a number of preinstalled "premium" channels from such content developers as Disney, America Online, CBS Sportsline, Money, and ABC News. Users can also install their own channels from developers that have their pages set up as channels.

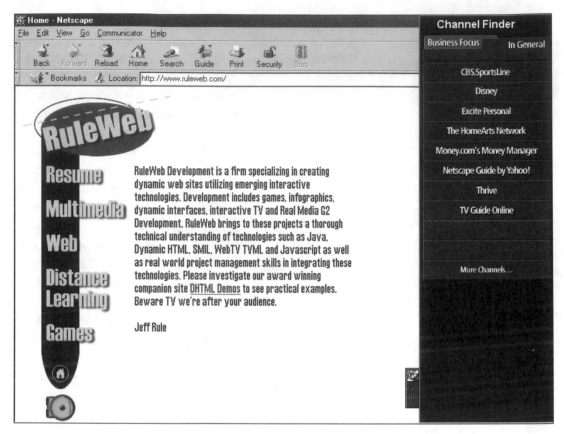

FIGURE 13-1. Netcaster channels

The Webtop

In addition to channels, Netscape allows you to present your
information via the webtop. The **webtop** consists of web pages
that are anchored to your desktop and that can act as the main
interface for your computer. By having a web-based interface take
over the computer desktop, companies can define a standard
"look and feel" for all of their interfaces, whether they are PC-,
Macintosh-, or UNIX-based.

The user views the webtop instead of the desktop interface,
and application windows float over the webtop as they would over

the standard desktop environment. A webtop is a complete user environment; users don't have to leave it to access other information from their systems, and following links from a webtop opens new windows instead of changing the underlying webtop. The webtop also allows users to continue working with applications while it displays "live" information continually, such as news services, static information, and forms for package-tracking services and search engines. Webtops can incorporate animated elements and crawling text (for example, stock tickers).

The webtop has not proved very popular as yet, but Netscape will continue to build on this idea with its next-generation web-based desktop, code-named Constellation. Constellation will act as a shell, allowing the user to log in on any computer running any operating system and receive the same desktop.

Defining Web Pages as Channels

Though both Netscape and Microsoft have raved about the potential for new immersive multimedia experiences and the "tremendous opportunity for developers," most developers have chosen to redefine their web pages as channels. This process is relatively simple and doesn't require a complete rework of an existing site, just the addition of some JavaScript code.

Netscape channels are built on the open standards of HTML and JavaScript 1.2. JavaScript 1.2 includes a new object called the "channel" object. This object allows channels to be defined. It enables you to control four key parameters:

- Channel description
- Channel delivery schedule
- Channel size
- Channel look and feel

Listing 13-1 gives the code for a simple channel.

LISTING 13-1. CREATION OF A NETSCAPE CHANNEL

```
1. <SCRIPT LANGUAGE="JavaScript1.2">
2.
3. function subscribe(){
4. var nc = components['netcaster']
5. var myChannel  = nc.getChannelObject();
6.
7. // Describe the channel
8. myChannel.url  = "http://www.ruleweb.com/dhtml/index.html";
9. myChannel.name = "DHTML Demos";
10. myChannel.desc = "Resource for Dynamic HTML Developers, Demos
    and Reviews of Software and Sites."
11.
12. // Set the schedule for push delivery
13. myChannel.intervalTime = 60
14.
15. // Establish guidelines for the cache size
16. myChannel.maxCacheSize = 2048000;
17. myChannel.depth = 2;
18.
19. // Set look and feel of the channel
20. myChannel.topHint = 0;
21. myChannel.leftHint = 0;
22. myChannel.widthHint = 200;
23. myChannel.heightHint = 200;
24. myChannel.mode = "window";
25.
26. // Add the channel
27. nc.addChannel(myChannel);
28. }
29.
30. </SCRIPT>
```

The body of the program consists of the following lines:

```
1.  <A HREF="#" onClick="subscribe(); return(false);">
2.  Add DHTML Demos Now!
3.  </a>
```

Let's analyze the important lines in Listing 13-1.

Lines 8–10:

```
8.  myChannel.url  = "http://www.ruleweb.com/dhtml/index.html";
9.  myChannel.name = "DHTML Demos";
10. myChannel.desc = "Resource for Dynamic HTML Developers, Demos
    and Reviews of Software and Sites."
```

Line 8 is the address of the initial web page that you wish to use in your channel. The page described here is often the same one in which you are placing the code. Think of it as the title page for your channel. Netscape encourages you to use DHTML and other technologies to make this page as interactive as possible. Instead, you may decide to add this code to your existing home page and worry about adding new technologies later.

Line 9 specifies your channel name—in this case **DHTML Demos**. You can name the page anything you like.

Line 10 includes a description of the site. It is a longer statement about the purpose of the site.

Line 13:

```
13. myChannel.intervalTime = 60
```

Line 13 describes how often the information should be pushed to the user. If the site includes late-breaking news, you might enter 60 (that is, every 60 minutes). For any interval of less than 24 hours, use the number of minutes. To update every day, enter −5; to update once a week, enter −6. (Strange, but true!)

Lines 15–17:

```
15. // Establish guidelines for the cache size
16. myChannel.maxCacheSize = 2048000;
17. myChannel.depth = 2;
```

In line 16, the **myChannel.maxCacheSize** parameter establishes how much room your site will occupy on the user's hard drive. The number is measured in bytes, where 1 megabyte = 1,024,000 bytes. In Listing 13-1, DHTML Demos asks for 2MB of space on the user's hard drive. This specification allows 2MB of information to be pushed to the user's hard drive. Remember, only information that has changed will actually be pushed. If you do not update your page, then no information will be pushed, even if the update time is set to every hour. The Netcaster component in Communicator reaches out to the server and checks for new information. If some is found, Netcaster downloads it. If nothing new is found, Netcaster waits and checks again in the time specified in line 13.

We know that Netcaster is downloading http://www.ruleweb.com/dhtml/index.html, but how much "deeper" into the site is it going? The **myChannel.depth** variable in line 17 allows you to set this level. DHTML Demos downloads the top level and then one more level deep. The structure set up in this example never has more than two levels; thus Netcaster should download the entire DHTML Demos site.

Line 24:

```
24. myChannel.mode = "window";
```

As noted earlier, there are two ways to present your channel: as a normal web page or as the desktop background. The webtop is one desktop background option.

Creating a Channel via Netscape's Wizard

Netscape has provided a wizard that allows you to create a Netcaster channel with ease. You simply answer some questions on a form, and the JavaScript and HTML code is generated for you. After you copy and paste this code into your web pages, you have a functioning channel. Push technology is actually much easier to develop than the experts would have you believe. Behind all the hype you can continue to use the same tools you've always used to develop web pages. Netscape has also provided a description of what the generated code actually means and how to modify it, found at http://developer.netscape.com/library/ examples/index.html?content=netcast/wizard/index.htm.

MICROSOFT CHANNELS

Underlying Technology

Microsoft has taken a slightly different route so as to produce a very similar result with push technology. It chose XML as the underlying technology for its channels. Although this standard is still in development, it promises to become as influential as HTML. XML is a centerpiece of Microsoft's emerging distributed application architecture (COM), which we discussed in Chapter 1.

Microsoft has taken a broader approach to push technology than Netscape, and a more complex one from the developer's point of view. As noted earlier, there have been many efforts to establish push applications in the market. Although the most successful to date has been Pointcast, each of these efforts has nevertheless provided a solution for a focused problem. Few, however, offer the flexibility needed to fill the larger role of providing an application standard for the overall problem of pushing or streaming content. Microsoft hopes to establish a standard to bring order to the chaotic push market and as part of its effort to build the next generation of push technology—distributed applications over the Internet.

Neither Netscape's nor Microsoft's channel format is true push technology. In fact, they are both really "smart pull." In a "smart pull" solution for "pushing" content, a client-side mechanism automatically schedules the HyperText Transfer Protocol (HTTP) content-pulling mechanism of regular web browsers,

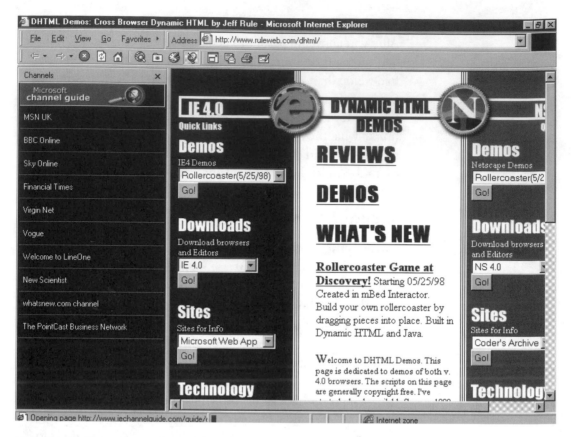

FIGURE 13-2. Internet Explorer 4 channels

presenting content pulled over HTTP to the user automatically, so that the user experiences pushed content. The underlying technology consists of HTTP as a transport protocol, combined with a scheduler that triggers requests and a user interface that presents regular HTML content that is automatically retrieved via HTTP. The resulting experience brings content to the user without requiring browsing to a site.

Of the various "smart pull" clients on the web today, some use simple web-crawl-based pull mechanisms to retrieve content—pulling the new content from a site using a scheduled crawl of every link starting from the home page. Most clients, however, use an application-specific directive file to program the scheduler to pull only the content needed to ensure that the user receives a "channel" experience. Regular HTTP polling is used to determine when new content is available and to pull it automatically for presentation to the user. In these more advanced clients, this file optimizes the "smart pull" mechanism, allowing content publishers to specify the schedule and exact set of resources that needs to be pulled.

Channel creation involves two other elements: the active desktop and screen savers. We will not discuss these elements in this book. If you'd like to read a good article on how to define them, check out the following source at Microsoft: http://www.microsoft.com/workshop/prog/ie4/channels/cdf2.htm.

Active Channel Content

You've created some great content. You've developed pull-down menus, animations, and 3-D rotating interfaces that are linked to demographic information and that morph to fit the user's every need. Now you want to turn it into an Internet Explorer 4 channel.

Branded Graphics

When your channel appears in the user's channel menus, you need to have several graphics to "brand" it so that the user can select it. Our example will include three images.

- A 194 × 32 pixel GIF image (Figure 13-3) appears in the channel pane, which displays all the channels to which the user has subscribed.
- An 80 × 32 pixel GIF image (Figure 13-4), similar to the 194 × 32 one, displays in the active desktop channel bar. This bar gives the selection of channels and sits on your desktop even when the browser is not open.

> **TIP**
> Users who are not connected to the Internet will not be able to view Java applets of Active X components. Remember this restriction when designing your channel.

FIGURE 13-3.
194 × 32 logo

FIGURE 13-4.
80 × 32 logo

FIGURE 13-5.
16 × 16 logo

- A 16 × 16 pixel ICO or GIF icon file (Figure 13-5) appears in the channel submenus of the channel pane. To create an .ico file, go to http://www.shareware.com and search for "icon editor"; you should see a wide variety of shareware and freeware. Pick one that converts BMP files to ICO files. You can create the original BMP image in the image editor of your choice. (I recommend Photoshop or Paint Shop Pro.)

CDF Files

It's time to take your first leap into XML. Microsoft has chosen to roll out Channel Definition Format (CDF) almost as an introduction to XML. Thus the developer can wade in slowly without having to worry about the entire spectrum of XML. Listing 13-2 gives the CDF file for my DHTML Demos. It shares some similarities with Netscape's definition.

LISTING 13-2. CDF FILE FOR DHTML DEMOS

```
1. <?XML VERSION="1.0" ENCODING="UTF-8"?>
2. <CHANNEL HREF="http://www.ruleweb.com/dhtml/index.html"
   LEVEL="1" PRECACHE="YES">
3. <ABSTRACT>DHTML Demos:  Developer Site with Real-World Dynamic
   HTML Demos and Reviews of DHTML Tools</ABSTRACT>

4. <TITLE>DHTML Demos</TITLE>
5. <LOGO HREF="http://www.ruleweb.com/dhtml/graphics/icon.jpg"
   STYLE="image" />
6. <LOGO HREF="http://www.ruleweb.com/dhtml/graphics/icon-w.jpg"
   STYLE="image-wide" />
```

```
7.  <LOGO HREF="http://www.ruleweb.com/dhtml/graphics/icon.ico"
    STYLE="icon" />

8.  <ITEM HREF="http://www.ruleweb.com/dhtml/html/whatsnew.html">
9.  <ABSTRACT>What's New at DHTML Demos</ABSTRACT>
10. <TITLE>What's New</TITLE>
11. </ITEM>

12. <ITEM HREF="http://www.ruleweb.com/dhtml/html/demos.html">
13. <ABSTRACT>Real-World Demos for Dynamic HTML</ABSTRACT>
14. <TITLE>Demos</TITLE>
15. </ITEM>

16. <ITEM HREF="http://www.ruleweb.com/dhtml/html/reviews.html">
17. <ABSTRACT>Reviews of Dynamic HTML Tools and Sites</ABSTRACT>
18. <TITLE>Reviews of Tools and Sites</TITLE>
19. </ITEM>

20. <SCHEDULE STARTDATE="1997-08-01">
21. <INTERVALTIME DAY="7" />
22. <EARLIESTTIME HOUR="0" />
23. <LATESTTIME HOUR="12" />
24. </SCHEDULE>

25. </CHANNEL>
```

After looking at the Netscape example, Listing 13-2 should be fairly easy to understand. As you can see, XML is much like HTML. XML merely allows you to define your own tags.

Lines 1–3:

```
1. <?XML VERSION="1.0" ENCODING="UTF-8"?>
2. <CHANNEL HREF="http://www.ruleweb.com/
   dhtml/index.html" LEVEL="1" PRECACHE="YES">
3. <ABSTRACT>DHTML Demos:  Developer Site with Real-World Dynamic
   HTML Demos and Reviews of DHTML Tools</ABSTRACT>
```

Line 1 defines this program as XML release 1.0. The character set is encoded as the default **UTF-8**. Don't worry about the character set: It will always be **UTF-8** for CDF files.

Line 2 provides the **CHANNEL** definition. Here is where you specify the URL of the first page of the channel. **LEVEL** is the number of levels deep that should be pushed to the client. On the DHTML Demos site, the first page would be pushed as well as one directory structure deep. **PRECACHE**, if omitted, is set to "yes." This variable controls whether the pushed pages are stored on the client machine. If it is set to "no," it eliminates much of the advantage of push technology.

In line 3, the **ABSTRACT** defines the purpose of your channel. This text will be displayed when the user mouses over the graphic for your site in the channel pane.

Lines 4–7:

```
4.  <TITLE>DHTML Demos</TITLE>
5.  <LOGO HREF="http://www.ruleweb.com/dhtml/graphics/icon.jpg"
    STYLE="image" />
6.  <LOGO HREF="http://www.ruleweb.com/dhtml/graphics/icon-w.jpg"
    STYLE="image-wide" />
7.  <LOGO HREF="http://www.ruleweb.com/dhtml/graphics/icon.ico"
    STYLE="icon" />
```

Line 4 provides the short title of your site. Line 5 defines where to find the 32 × 80 GIF/JPG imaging discussed in the section "Branded Graphics." Line 6 defines where to find the 32 × 194 GIF/JPG image, and line 7 defines where to find the 16 × 16 icon.

> **TIP**
> ......
> Don't forget to add the "/" at the end of the tag.

Lines 8–11:

```
8.  <ITEM HREF="http://www.ruleweb.com/dhtml/html/whatsnew.html">
9.  <ABSTRACT>What's New at DHTML Demos</ABSTRACT>
10. <TITLE>What's New</TITLE>
11. </ITEM>
```

Line 8 includes the subheadings for your channel. These items appear when the user double-clicks the graphic in the channel pane. They are categories for your web site. Notice that DHTML Demos contains three items: **What's New**, **Demos**, and **Review of Tools and Sites**. We'll explain only the first one. In line 8, you include the URL to your first item's page. Line 9 includes the **ABSTRACT**. Just as you defined the abstract for the overall site, you define the abstract for the subchannel.

In line 10, **TITLE** is the title of the subchannel. In this case, it's **What's New**.

Line 11 closes the **ITEM** tag.

Lines 20–24:

```
20. <SCHEDULE STARTDATE="1997-08-01">
21. <INTERVALTIME DAY="7" />
22. <EARLIESTTIME HOUR="0" />
23. <LATESTTIME HOUR="12" />
24. </SCHEDULE>
```

Line 20 gives the date on which the scheduling starts.

In line 21, we see that this channel will be updated every seven days. The interval time can be set to **DAY**, **HOUR**, or **MIN**. Don't update more often than necessary, because it jams up the Internet.

In line 22, **EARLIESTTIME** is the earliest time in the day that the push can occur. By setting a timeframe lasting several hours, you ensure that the web server isn't hit with all requests at once. Instead, the requests are spaced out over the times defined by **EARLIESTTIME** and **LATESTTIME**. At Discovery, we have had some problems with these parameters working correctly on a Silicon Graphics server.

In line 23, **LATESTTIME** defines the end of the period in which the push update occurs.

Line 24 ends the schedule. We then end the channel definition in line 25.

Once the CDF file, graphics, and content are in place, you need a way to activate them. This process requires a link on your page. The JavaScript snippet given below determines whether your browser is Internet Explorer 4. If it is, it takes you to the CDF file and starts the subscription process. If your browser is not Internet Explorer 4, it takes you to an Internet Explorer 4 download page. You can then change the URL for the CDF file to point to your own CDF file and include a graphic file or text for the user to click on.

```
<A HREF="javascript:navigator.
userAgent.indexOf('MSIE 4')>-1?
location.href='http://www.ruleweb.com/
dhtml/dhtml.cdf':
location.href='http://www.microsoft.com/
ie/ie40/download/?/ie/ie40/download/
redirect.htm';
">
<IMG SRC="graphics/addChan.gif"
WIDTH=136 HEIGHT=20 BORDER=0>
</A>
```

SUMMARY

Push technology has not proved as popular as was originally anticipated. Push was intended as a method to deliver web-based multimedia content to the end user. By having push occur automatically, perhaps in the middle of the night, the user avoided the download times associated with high-bandwidth web content. Most content developers, however, remain leery of producing expensive immersive content for the web in light of the virtual collapse of the economics of the CD-ROM market.

Many sites have produced, at best, an introductory screen that takes advantage of new technologies such as DHTML. This single screen does not need to be pushed. Content providers will need to see standards for this new technology before they will be willing to invest the time and money necessary to create immersive content similar to CD-ROM.

LINKS

Netscape
Defining Netcaster Channels in JavaScript
http://developer.netscape.com/news/viewsource/
     angus_dncjs.html

Netscape Netcaster—Adding Channels
http://developer.netscape.com/library/examples/netcast/
     add_channel.html

Building a Channel
http://developer.netscape.com/library/documentation/tools/
     devguide/chan.htm

Microsoft
Creating Active Channels
http://www.microsoft.com/msdn/sdk/inetsdk/help/delivery/
     authoring/active_channels.htm

CDF Reference
http://www.microsoft.com/msdn/sdk/inetsdk/help/delivery/
     references/CDF.htm#content_cdfref

Beyond the Basics (CDF Channels)
http://www.microsoft.com/workshop/prog/ie4/channels/
     cdf2.htm22

THE VERSION 5 BROWSERS:
A SNEAK PEAK

BACKGROUND

By the time you read this book, the version 5 browsers will be hitting the street. In many ways, the new browsers have begun to diverge in terms of their main focus. Internet Explorer 5's interface remains much the same, but some of the underlying technology has undergone an evolutionary upgrade. Netscape Communicator 5 will be the result of the work being carried out by Mozilla, an organization set up by Netscape that freely distributes the Communicator source code. This open policy gives developers and programmers everywhere the ability to change the code and make improvements. No one really knows what this radical experiment in communal software engineering will yield.

Internet Explorer 5

Internet Explorer 5 is aimed at the next generation of web applications. Microsoft is making development easier for designers and programmers by making it simpler to implement Dynamic HTML. The version 5 browser is built on many of the standards approved by W3C. It supports Dynamic HTML, the W3C DOM, Cascading Style Sheets 2.0 (CSS2), PICS, XML, CDF,

Active X, Java, and an open scripting model for technologies like JavaScript or ECMAScript.

Most of the new features are intended to persuade developers to support Internet Explorer 5 as the main interface for future web applications. Let's look at some of the new features that Microsoft is using to win support.

Dynamic HTML Behaviors

Dynamic HTML behaviors are an unapproved extension to CSS2. Using such behaviors, the web developer can separate the Dynamic HTML code from the HTML code by applying a Dynamic HTML behavior to an object on the screen. The behavior is stored in an external file and then applied to many different objects on the screen. This approach is similar to the way that you might apply a style type to text using the `<span>` tag. The `<span>` tag can be reused many times in the document without explicitly stating it every time. Likewise, if you have a DHTML behavior (such as animation), you can apply it to many graphics on the screen without rewriting the DHTML behavior for each graphic. We'll see a demonstration of this ability in the "Examples" section later in this chapter.

Embedded XML Support

Internet Explorer 5 supports the XML 1.0 standard from W3C. Developers can mix HTML and XML in the same document as well as access the XML DOM. XML can also be laid out on the screen using CSS2. (See Chapter 3 for more information on CSS2.)

Drag and Drop

The version 5 browser supports full application-level drag-and-drop events. The user can drag between frames on a web page or between a web page and an application, such as Word. Both the web page and the application must support Win-32-based IDropTarget and IDragSource COM interfaces. Thus this feature will work only on Windows 95, 98, and NT machines. As we discussed back in Chapter 8, this kind of functionality could revolutionize e-commerce and Internet gaming.

Cascading Style Sheets 2

CSS2 support will contain some additional unsupported tags, such as those involved in integrating DHTML behaviors. CSS2 also supports the layout of XML documents.

Dynamic Properties

In CSS, the values are set to scalar values; in other words, they are set to an exact number or property. For example, the width of a graphic may be set to 250; the color of text may be set to blue. **Dynamic properties** allow the CSS properties to react to the environmental conditions in which the page is being displayed. If the screen has a resolution of 800×600 pixels, then the browser might use an 18-point font; if the resolution is 640×480, it might use a 12-point font. Essentially you will be able to perform math operations on any CSS property, using Excel-like expressions. We'll see an example of these properties in the "Examples" section later in this chapter.

Persistence

Web pages have become increasingly customizable. You load a page, open some hierarchy menus, highlight some choices, and fill out some forms; when you return to the page, though, all the changes have been erased and need to be entered again. Until now, you had to store this information in cookies or in a database. Internet Explorer 5 allows four types of data persistence:

Save Snapshot: This method allows you to save a page in HTML exactly the way it looked after you finished modifying it. This feature can be especially useful in an intranet or web application environment. Imagine that you filled out an expense report over the web. Each time you accessed it, the form changed only slightly. Using this method, you could have the form retain the data between visits and make only the minor changes necessary before resubmitting.

User Date Persistence: This feature is an XML-based storage methodology for saving large amounts of user data. If you have a large volume of data to save from some point in time (for example, your favorite sports teams' scores for the last ten years), then you can use persistence rather than cookies.

Save History: This XML-based storage methodology allows you to save history data.

Save Favorites: This XML-based storage methodology allows you to save favorites data.

HTML Applications

As you may have noticed, Dynamic HTML allows you to build nearly all the functions of an application. You can create pull-down menus, forms, animation, dynamic text, cut-and-paste operations, and drag-and-drop features. Web applications are becoming increasingly prominent, and more people are becoming application builders. But do you always want to run your application on the web in a browser's window? Wouldn't it be nice to build the application in HTML and then package it as a stand-alone application? Internet Explorer 5 gives you an opportunity to do so. After the developer has finished debugging the application in HTML, he or she can save the files with an HTA (hypertext application) extension. This idea is still in development by Microsoft, but the HTA will appear in its own window, just like an application, without the menus and buttons seen in the browser.

Netscape Communicator 5

Netscape has released its Communicator browser code as freeware, with a few restrictions. Developers are free to modify and use the code in any way they like, but they must pass the code for these changes back to Netscape for potential inclusion in later versions of Communicator. This freeware development model has worked well with the LINUX operating system and with the Apache web server, but it remains to be seen how it will work with a commercial product.

When Netscape decided to release its browser code to the public, it stepped away from the rapid upgrade path the company

> **TIP**
> ....
> Netscape has released an interim version of Communicator known as version 4.5. This version doesn't contain any Dynamic HTML enhancements.

had been following. It also distanced itself from several new technologies. Because of this change in direction and financial problems of the company, only the vaguest outlines have emerged of what will be included in Communicator 5. The most up-to-date information can be found at the Mozilla site (http://www.mozilla.org) or at this book's web site. Keeping this uncertainty in mind, let's look at what we do know about the version 5 browser.

NGLayout Engine

The part of Communicator 5 that most affects Dynamic HTML developers is the NGLayout engine (Next-Generation Layout Engine). This element decides how the HTML, XML, and DHTML code should be drawn to the screen. It includes all of the HTML information and the DOM.

Document Object Model

Netscape has stated that Communicator 5 will be a blend of Communicator 4 and W3C DOM Level 1. According to Mozilla,

> The aim is to provide compatibility with the Communicator 4.0 event model as well as the W3C DOM event model standard (which is as yet unspecified). Ideally, these two models will not be mutually exclusive.
> — http://www.mozilla.org/newlayout/dom-roadmap.html

This compatibility will mean that many more objects can be manipulated using Dynamic HTML. Unlike Communicator 4, version 5 will allow all HTML objects to be manipulated even after they are drawn to the screen.

Cascading Style Sheets

Communicator 5 will fully support CSS1 and will have a partial implementation of CSS2. The extent of the latter support is not known.

Compatibility with Internet Explorer

Compatibility is mentioned several times on the Mozilla site. Realistically, Communicator will probably be more compatible with version 4 of Internet Explorer than with version 5. By exposing all HTML objects to the DOM, Communicator 5 will closely resemble Internet Explorer 4. In the meantime, however, Microsoft has also been making changes to its browser. For its part, Netscape has been focusing energy on tying Communicator into its Netcenter web site. Thus some of the company's development energy is being spent on integration, not new development.

TECHNICAL LIMITS
AND UNDERLYING TECHNOLOGY

The new features in both of these version 5 browsers will require faster machines. Internet Explorer 5 will be tied more closely to the Windows platform than ever before. Such functionality as drag and drop will pull directly from the Windows architecture.

Compatibility will continue to be a key issue. As a general rule, compatibility always seems to lag one browser generation behind. Both version 5 browsers are expected to be compatible to the level of Internet Explorer 4. It is against the business interests of both Netscape and Microsoft to make their browsers 100% compatible, because there would be no way to differentiate them in the market.

Communicator 5 releases for UNIX and especially for Macintosh will probably appear much later than the other PC-based releases. In particular, Netscape has had problems finding Macintosh developers who are willing to donate their time to the effort.

EXAMPLES

No code samples have been released for Communicator 5 yet, so the following examples are all based on the developer's release of Internet Explorer 5. The code may be subject to change if Microsoft makes changes to the browser. The DHTML Demos web site (http://www.ruleweb.com/dhtml) will contain the latest demonstrations for both browsers.

Dynamic HTML Behaviors

Listing 14-1 provides an example of a Dynamic HTML behavior.

LISTING 14-1. DYNAMIC HTML BEHAVIOR

```
1.  <html>
2.  <head>

3.  <style>
4.  .mouser{behavior:url(mouse.sct);}
5.  </style>

6.  </head>
7.  <body>

8.  <div id=text class=mouser> This text changes color and cursor
    when rolled over and the font size increases when clicked.
9.  </div>

10. </body>
11. </html>
```

The important thing to notice in this example is line 4, which you may recognize as a style sheet. In this line, however, we are using a new property called a **behavior**. This new CSS functionality has been submitted to W3C by Microsoft, but has not been approved yet. The **behavior** allows a reusable script to be attached to an object and then reused multiple times with the same scripting code. It is attached to any HTML object by adding the class (**class=mouser**) shown in line 8. Any HTML object that has this class attached gains the **mouser** functionality.

The scriptlet is kept in an external SCT file. ("SCT" is an abbreviation for "Scriptlet.") By separating the scripting and the HTML, we have taken one more step toward separating the fields of design, content provision, and programming. CSS allowed us to separate content and layout, and now programming can be separated into reusable scriptlets. This encapsulation of pieces of web development will lead to specialization in web development and allow web pages to make the transition into a true production process. No longer will the same person have to provide content, design, and programming. While some of us might miss being a "jack of all trades," this step is necessary to move web development into the mainstream media.

Behaviors can perform a variety of functions:

- They can create and manipulate new attributes and methods on the HTML element to which they are attached, so that these characteristics appear to the document author as standard attributes and methods on the element.
- They can start custom events, so that the events appear to the document author as standard events on the HTML element.
- They can access the element to which they are attached, and therefore access the entire document through the document's object model.
- They can catch (find a user interaction, such as a mouseclick) events from within the HTML document.

Now let's examine the SCT file that we attached as a behavior. This file, shown in Listing 14-2, is much like an external CSS file.

LISTING 14-2. SCT FILE

```
1. <scriptlet id="mouse">
2. <implements id="Behavior" type="Behavior" default />
3. <script language="jscript">
4. attachEvent("onclick", event_onclick);
5. attachEvent("onmouseover", event_onmouseover);
6. attachEvent("onmouseout", event_onmouseout);

7. function event_onmouseover(){
8. style.cursor = "hand";
```

```
 9. style.color = "red";}

10. function event_onmouseout(){
11. style.cursor = "";
12. style.fontWeight = "";
13. style.fontSize = "";
14. style.color = "black";}

15. function event_onclick(){
16. style.fontWeight = "bold";
17. style.fontSize = "24";
18. style.color = "green";}
19. </script>
20. </scriptlet>
```

Lines 1–6:

Line 1 names the scriptlet. In this case, it is called **mouse** to show that it reacts to mouse events in the HTML document. The **implements** tag allows us to attach custom properties, methods, and events. In this case, we have attached three events: **event_onclick**, **event_onmouseover**, and **event_onmouseout**. These custom events correspond to the mouse events with which you are already familiar.

Lines 7–20:

The remaining lines look much like a regular script. On the **event_onmouseover** event, the hand cursor appears and the text turns red. On the **event_onmouseout** event, the cursor, font weight, font color, and font size return to their original conditions. On the **event_onclick** event, the text is made bold, 24 point, and green.

This simple demonstration only hints at the enormous power associated with being able to attach this scriptlet file to many different HTML files and to many different places in each HTML file. By storing your scripts in one file, any changes need to be made only once to affect the scriptlet's use in many different places.

Dynamic Properties

Dynamic properties allow the CSS properties to be set up as expressions rather than absolute values. Using equations similar to Excel expressions, you can dynamically change the properties based on environmental conditions, such as browser window width; alternatively, you might make the properties of one HTML object relate to another object. For example, if the user mouses over some text, the text might get bigger. You could have an associated picture increase in size as well.

In Listing 14-3, the font size changes with the width of the browser window.

LISTING 14-3. DYNAMIC PROPERTIES—LINKING FONT SIZE TO BROWSER WINDOW WIDTH

```
1.  <html>
2.  <body>
3.  <h1
4.  style="
5.  font-family: arial;
6.  text-align: center;
7.  font-size: function(document.body.clientWidth / 12)">
8.  Dynamic HTML Demos
9.  </h1>
10. Resize the window to watch the text above change size
    dynamically.
11. </body>
12. </html>
```

As you can see, all of the action happens in line 7. The font size is set to an expression that is one-twelfth of the width of the browser window. Try this technique on your own with more complex scripting, such as that involving modifications, image widths and heights, and be sure to check DHTML Demos for the latest Internet Explorer 5 demos.

SUMMARY

This chapter is by no means a comprehensive overview of Internet Explorer 5 or Netscape Communicator 5. Both browsers are still evolving. It should allow you a sneak peek into the future of web browsing, however, and give you a head start in preparing for it. Netscape and Microsoft have chosen to take different directions with their version 5 browsers. Microsoft is charging ahead with web applications and with the emerging standards from W3C, such as XML and CSS2. Netscape, while still conforming to standards and providing at least partial support of these new standards, is working on the usability of its browser through features such as faster searching and a better user interface. By getting an early look, you can be ready when these new developments hit the mainstream.

LINKS

Internet Explorer 5 Demos
http://www.microsoft.com/workshop/
  c-frame.htm?899675362970#/gallery/samples/default.asp

Internet Explorer 5 Drag-and-Drop Example
http://www.microsoft.com/gallery/samples/ie50/dragndrop/
  items_htm.htm

Internet Explorer 5 Fly-in Example
http://www.microsoft.com/gallery/samples/ie50/flyflyin.htm

Netscape Communicator 5 (Mozilla.org)
http://www.mozilla.org

THE FUTURE

From its humble origins in Netscape 2.0, JavaScript has come a long way. It has made the jump from a marginally useful browser detector and timestamp creator to a full-fledged programming language. What will the future hold? In this chapter, we'll take a look at how changes in technology will affect web developers, users, future technologies, and uses of the web.

WEB DESIGNERS

Web design has come a long way since Netscape 1.0. HTML, as a standard, has been relatively static since Netscape 3. Although there have been some additions, they have mainly been made to help HTML tie into newer technologies, such as Java or CSS. With W3C's final approval of HTML 4.0, the rapid evolution of HTML is nearly complete. With the W3C standard in place, common HTML development will increasingly move to "What You See Is What You Get" (WYSIWYG) tools for development. Such tools will become more sophisticated and begin to generate clearer, more readable code. Macromedia Dreamweaver represents a step in this direction. You will be able to edit the code, but many web designers will no longer need to do so.

The fact that you purchased this book shows that you are aware of these changes and realize that a job as an HTML developer may not be an option forever. Web developers need to take the next logical step into JavaScript and Dynamic HTML. Fortunately, this step is an easy one compared with jumping directly into programming.

The existence of the View Source button has done as much to popularize web development as any other force. HTML developers need to take advantage of this valuable resource to look at the JavaScript and Dynamic HTML that exists on the web and learn from it.

Dynamic HTML is just the first step in web programming. Web development is gradually going to evolve to become more like other types of programming. Client-side code such as JavaScript may well expand to include VBScript and other languages. Along with this increasing level of programming-language difficulty, there will be new tools to help in development. Professional programmers don't sit down with SimpleText or Notepad to do their programming. Instead, they use tools like Metrowerk's CodeWarrior or Microsoft's Visual C++. These visual development environments automate many of the mundane aspects of coding and increase output. Expect tools such as Microsoft's Visual InterDev and NetObject's Fusion to grow into similar tools for web development.

Web development will increasingly focus on distributed applications. Microsoft's Distributed interNet Applications (DNA) architecture is all about building web applications that tie into existing data sources and applications. Many companies are working to make their data resources directly available to their workers at other sites, their suppliers, and even to their customers. Someone must build the interface to make all these resources available on the web. That someone should be you.

Tying into a database can seem like a daunting task when all you've known is HTML and client-side JavaScript. Nevertheless, it is an important next step to take in furthering your career. There are some steps you can take to ease this transition. Tying into a database requires some sort of middleware product. Some of the easier ones to use are described below.

Allaire Cold Fusion (Sun and Windows NT)

Many PC web developers do their development in Allaire Home-site, a Windows-based HTML editor. The same company makes another product, called Cold Fusion, that allows the user to insert elements from a database using simple HTML-like tags. In fact, Cold Fusion tags are built directly into Homesite. If you want to make a simple query to the database, you use friendly tags like the following:

```
<CFQUERY DATASOURCE="united"
NAME="GetPatientDetails">
  Select *  From Patients Where
  Patient_ID = #CheckPatient.Patient_ID#
</CFQUERY>
```

This example does the following: It looks in the database **united**, finds the subheading **GetPatientDetails**, and reads out all the fields for a certain patient ID. (Note: The ID was entered in an HTML form and submitted.) The selected information is then written to the screen.

```
<CFOUTPUT Query="GetPatientDetails">
#FirstName# #LastName#, all of us here
at United Health are wishing you a
healthy day.
```

In these lines, the patient's first and last names are written to the screen to personalize it.

You might notice that this code is a lot like HTML code. The resulting pages communicate with the Cold Fusion application server, which pulls the information from the database and puts it into the web page.

Macromedia Backstage (Windows NT)

Macromedia has sadly neglected the Backstage product of late. The company has chosen to focus on multimedia development and has let this product sit with few updates. Backstage provides a point-and-click interface for tying into databases through Microsoft's ODBC. Much like Cold Fusion, it uses proprietary HTML-like tags to pull the information from the database and insert it in the web page. Backstage's advantage is that it works in a WYSIWYG environment.

As you can see from the previously given examples, building distributed applications doesn't have to be hard-core coding. With so much riding on on-line commerce, intranets, and extranets, new application development environments are rapidly emerging to make web applications a point-and-click reality.

Having a back-end database offers a way to separate the data from the document structure. Imagine having 10,000 patients in a database and then creating a separate page for each one of them. No way! By using a page layout and plugging in the data, you can effectively separate layout and content. If you've been lingering on W3C's every word, then this tactic might sound familiar—it sounds like XML.

XML: Data Just the Way You Want It

XML has been described as a universal format for data on the web. It allows developers to deliver rich, structured data to the client. In the future, XML may be generated by a database and passed to the client. The user will then be able to manipulate this data on his or her own machine, without going back to the server to request more data. The main demand on servers is the number of requests that they must process. By offloading this task onto the user's machine, the server doesn't have to work as hard and can serve more users. On the client machine, the user can manipulate the data in many different forms. Sort in alphabetically, sort by price, look at only products with a four-star rating—the user can do it all without ever recontacting the server. But if XML is the data, what provides the document structure?

CSS2 and XSL: Giving a Backbone to the Data

Both CSS and regular HTML can be used as a structure for XML data, but they may not provide the flexibility to reformat and sort the data. To accomplish this goal, the developer may need to resort to two new technologies just coming into focus at W3C. CSS2, which was discussed briefly in Chapter 3, is mainly aimed at identifying alternative media types and dealing with layout in non-computer-based web browers. It may also be adjusted to provide a flexible structure for XML data.

Another contender has also recently emerged to vie for this title. Although **XSL (Extensible Stylesheet Language)** may have initially appeared redundant to CSS, it now appears to fill a legitimate need. XSL allows the author to apply formatting operations to XML elements. The following is a quote from Microsoft's XSL site (http://www.microsoft.com/xml/xsl/tutorial/what.htm):

> CSS is a style sheet language that may also be used with XML. But with CSS, the basic structure of the document cannot be dramatically altered. CSS essentially maps each XML element into a single display object with certain display characteristics (or properties). XSL, in comparison, allows a single XML source element to be mapped into a more complex hierarchy of display objects. For instance, XSL can add a legal disclaimer to the end of a document, generate a table of contents, and calculate and display chapter and section numbers. In addition, XSL is made extensible through script, flow object macros (not yet implemented), and extensible flow object types (not yet implemented).

As you can see, the future of web development will involve a number of standards that will serve as the backbone for distributed web applications, Internet commerce, database access, and on-line gaming. With all this new information, what will the future web user expect to find on the web and how will he or she use this information?

WEB USERS

Did you ever become so caught up in a new technology that you forgot that only 5% of the end users would be able to view your product? I know I have. I remember creating early Shockwave movies that were as large as 10MB—when the average modem could handle only 9600 bps. There was no way that anyone could download that monster. Sitting at the end of a fast Internet connection, developers sometimes forget what it's like to wait three minutes to download a graphics-heavy page. Developers must always keep users' needs in mind. What does the user come to the web to find? More importantly, what will attract an increasing percentage of the population?

Web Lifestyle

The other day, I was talking on the phone with a friend who was going to work on a project in Como, Italy. On the way there, he was staying in London for a week to meet with his team. During our conversation, he mentioned that he didn't know where Como was located in Italy. Without even breaking stride, I brought up Digital's AltaVista Search Engine, typed in "Como Italy," and got back a number of responses. The best one was in Italian, so I translated it using AltaVista's translation capabilities. The translation was rough, but it was adequate to tell my friend where the town was located and how close it was to some major cities in Italy. Moments later, we were talking about the weather in London. I brought relevant information up from the Weather Channel site (http://www.weather.com). My friend works for a major accounting firm doing reengineering. Although he owns a laptop and is up to date on most of the latest technology, this rapid access to information amazed him.

"Information at your fingertips" is what the web is all about. Night or day, anywhere in the world, your customers can find out information about your company, send e-mail with questions, and even order products from many large companies without ever contacting anyone. This kind of access to information is what draws people to the web. As an increasing number of databases are hooked into the web, the amount of information will only continue to grow.

With so much information on-line, however, it becomes difficult to filter through it to find what you need. Search engines are one solution, but the existing engines need to be made more user-friendly. New English-language query technology is making it easier to conduct a search.

Despite these myriad new technologies, most people prefer to get their information from a name they can trust. When I was trying to find data about the weather in London, I didn't run an AltaVista search—I went straight to the Weather Channel because I knew the site would have up-to-date information. No matter how good the search engine, brand names will still carry weight. The challenge for web developers is to make finding this information as easy as possible.

E-commerce has been a buzzword for the last year and a half. This past Christmas, I did nearly three-quarters of my shopping on-line and had the gifts delivered directly to my home. I bought clothes at Lands End, books from Amazon.com, CDs from CD-NOW, software from Egg Head, and medieval replicas from Design Toscano. Many people remain reluctant to pass their credit card information over the Internet, however. There are good reasons for this fear, and any user should always verify that the seller is using an encrypted server. On the other hand, most people wouldn't think twice about giving their credit cards to a worker at a restaurant. People need time to adjust to buying things over the web, and developers need to make the entire process more user-friendly. It helps that major names, such as IBM and Microsoft, are getting into e-commerce. IBM may not be a hot, flashy Silicon Valley startup, but it will be a trusted name in protecting credit card information.

Gaming is another hot topic on the Internet. Many big names, such as Sony and Microsoft, have already jumped into the fray and are heavily promoting their gaming sites.

Sony has banked on moving many of its game-show franchises onto the web at its gaming site, The Station (http://www.station.sony.com/). Here you can play the game shows you see on television, including "Wheel of Fortune" and "Jeopardy." This merger of television and the web is being fueled by Sony's creation of a new division, Sony Online Entertainment, which will focus on the on-line gaming market. Sony passed the 1 million mark for members in March 1998. The company has intelligently used proven brand names on the web. It is cashing in by serving people who watch these game shows and think they could do better than the contestants. Game-show-style games have proven a natural for an advertising-driven model, as they have natural breaks in the action between rounds where advertising can be shown.

Although Microsoft is not traditionally a media company, it has put together a number of consumer-oriented sites, including The Internet Gaming Zone (http://www.zone.com/asp/default.asp). This site features a few name brands, such as Scrabble and other classic games from Hasbro Interactive. It also features entertainment brands, such as LucasArts Entertainment's Jedi Knight: Dark Forces II. Microsoft has also capitalized on its limited gaming offers by creating an on-line version of Age of Empires.

Until recently, board games and strategy games were better suited to the web because of slow connections. Action games or "twitch" games didn't respond well over the Internet. Nothing is more frustrating than seeing a monster and having to wait two seconds before your gun reacts! Latency has been a major issue, but one that has been solved. Real-time encounters for games like Quake and Fighter Ace occur on the web thousands of times each day.

Game communities are the fastest-growing and tightest-knit groups on the web today. Some companies, such as Origin Software, are creating even tighter communities of users by creating games that never end. Origin has taken the most popular role-playing game of all time on-line with Ultima Online (http://www.owo.com/). In this virtual world, you can behave any way you want. You can form clans for protection, set up a shop, or travel. The world is so large that it would take ten hours to walk across if you held down a movement key and traveled in one direction. It contains 200 million square virtual feet of space with

12 towns and 7 dungeons. Ultima Online is a subscription game for which users pay a certain price per month. Unending games such as this one build strong user communities and may well represent the future for on-line gaming.

Services

It is a recent revelation to most web developers that content may not be king on the Internet. People rarely come to the Internet to read long articles, largely because reading from a screen is not a pleasant experience. For a long time pundits have argued that consumers would "get used to" this sensation, but I disagree. Like many people, I will always choose a print copy of the newspaper over an on-line version.

People come to the web for services. They come for all the reasons mentioned earlier and they come to send e-mail, book a flight, check product information, and use other services. From a design standpoint, it is important to remember that creating a web page is more than putting a lengthy written brochure on the web. You should rewrite the materials to be brief and ensure that the site is visually appealing. As you take the next step in web development, remember why your users come to your site.

TECHNOLOGY

Two conflicting forces drive the web. One force seeks to tear the web apart with proprietary technology. The other attempts to reach a large audience and keeps standards in place. These conflicting forces are what will shape the future of the web.

Balkanization

Proprietary technology is not always what rips the web apart. Certainly, incorporating inconsistent HTML tags or different DOMs can create incompatibility between browsers, but you may look back on these problems with fondness when you see the coming schism. In a recent article in *Feed Magazine*, Mark Pesce discussed how Microsoft is planning to tie its browser directly to its operating system. According to the article, Internet Explorer 5 will be capable of displaying 3-D objects on web pages. This technology will be tied to Direct X, a Windows-only technology. Direct X is also tied directly to Intel processors. Thus Internet Explorer 5 customers will experience distinctly different content when they enter an enhanced page than will Netscape users. Microsoft is being savvy by writing these extensions in XML, a W3C-accepted standard.

Clearly, standards and compatibility are not always synonymous. For Java, for example, Microsoft has introduced classes that tie directly into the Windows operating system. When Java is written to these classes, it becomes incompatible with other operating systems. Many have claimed that Microsoft intends to destroy Java as a universal standard for cross-platform compatibility. Such a standard could pose a threat to the existing Windows de facto standard. Is Microsoft "balkanizing," or is the company merely innovating, building on the strengths of its operating system? Whatever the answer to this question, it is clear that a fine line is being drawn.

Business Will Keep Us Together

The fragmentation of the web can sound scary for web developers. A counterforce, however, works to keep the web compatible on at least a minimal level. Business has discovered the web in a big way. The *Fortune* 1000 companies have all developed web sites, and many of them already have e-commerce sites running. Others have moved into personalizing the sites and gathering user demographics. These businesses want to be able to reach users, no matter which browser a particular customer has. It simply costs too much to build two web sites, one for Microsoft and one for Netscape.

Microsoft makes most of its money selling server and operating system software to big business. The company is not about to push a totally incompatible product. Thus Internet Explorer 5 and Netscape 5, no matter what enhancements they may possess, will maintain a certain base level of functionality that is compatible with all browsers.

SUMMARY

We've looked at some of the possible scenarios for the next few years of web development. It is very difficult to forecast the outlook for any field that is only a few years old. Who knows—perhaps HDTV and digital set-top boxes will overtake computers as the preferred way to access the Internet. The one certainty is that the Internet will persist in one form or another and that the demand for people to create for it will increase. I hope this book has aided your next step into a career with great prospects.

LINKS

Some advanced Dynamic HTML sites for you to enjoy are listed below.

Arcade Games
http://www1.nisiq.net/~jimmeans/
http://www.t3.rim.or.jp/~naoto/

Star Thruster 100
http://members.xoom.com/dynduo/starthruster/

Asteroids
http://www.microsoft.com/ie/ie40/demos/asteroids.htm

DYNAMIC HTML AUTHORING TOOLS

In this book, we have often compared Dynamic HTML and CD-ROM authoring. Dynamic HTML may lead to a revolution in how content is authored for the web. Using a combination of efficient Dynamic HTML with increasing bandwidth, developers should be able to create applications and dynamic storytelling that rivals those possible with CD-ROM. Internet Explorer 4 has delivered many of the raw tools necessary for this revolution to happen. Netscape 4 makes it somewhat harder, but Netscape 5 promises to achieve parity with Internet Explorer 4 and perhaps surpass it.

Nevertheless, one of Netscape's most promising technologies, Gemini, was recently canceled. This tool, which was written in Java, held out the possibility of unsurpassed multimedia performance. As Netscape noted, Gemini offered

> Content with no limit. With Netscape's new rendering and layout engine, code-named Gemini, users and developers will be able to create documents that rival the best paper printouts. Gemini will also facilitate the creation of interactive and dynamic content, providing a richer and more compelling user experience than CD-ROM multimedia titles provide.

Unfortunately, Netscape's financial problems caused the company to shelve development of this technology.

When I left CD-ROM development, several great development tools were in their fourth, fifth, or sixth release. These tools had been thoroughly refined, and their user interfaces made them easy to program.

I'm partial to Macromedia tools, especially Authorware and Director. Macromedia has already produced the superior Dreamweaver tool that speeds web development. Its Director product now supports Java output. Macromedia has also discussed altering Director to output Dynamic HTML. Director and Authorware output of Dynamic HTML, however, lies in the future.

Let's look at some of the tools that currently export Dynamic HTML.

MBED INTERACTOR

Coding Dynamic HTML by hand can be a time-consuming process, especially if you are attempting to achieve cross-browser compatibility or full-fledged applications or interactive stories. There is only one tool on the market that I consider to be a full-fledged authoring tool for Dynamic HTML—mBed Interactor (Figure A-1).

Many companies have tried to retrofit their products to output Dynamic HTML. They have met with varying levels of success. mBed has successfully adapted its tool because it was originally conceived as a web-based authoring tool, unlike products such as Macromedia Director, which were CD-ROM tools long before Shockwave emerged. Interactor originally created web-based multimedia using a plug-in and movies called mbedlets. Over time, the company has added Java output and Dynamic HTML output.

At Discovery Channel, we typically create one piece of content in Interactor. We then save it as Dynamic HTML optimized for Netscape, Dynamic HTML optimized for Internet Explorer 4,

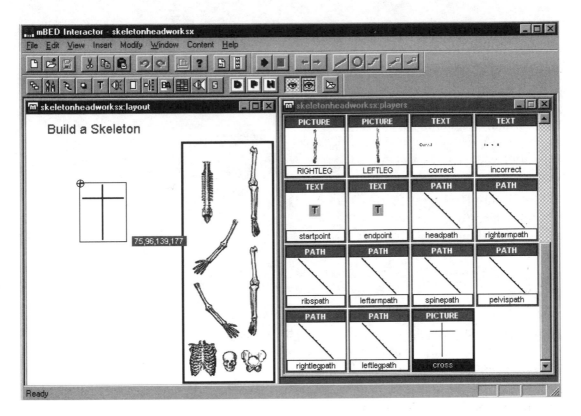

FIGURE A-1. mBed Interactor interface

and Java for older browsers. Imagine the time it would take to create all three of these pieces individually!

Interactor does not attempt to create a universal mbedlet that can play in any browser. The company has accepted the inevitable differences between different browsers and has tailored its tool to create optimized content for each.

The scripting behind each page is stored in a 20K JavaScript file that accompanies the page. This massive JavaScript file contains all the functions needed to run the Dynamic HTML presentation you are creating. Although this file holds a great deal of JavaScript, it is much smaller than any Java runtime or Shockwave piece you are liable to develop.

Mbedlets are based on a library of built-in multimedia players that include the following:

- Sprites
- Text
- Paths (for animation)
- Buttons
- Boxes
- Sound (including real audio support)
- Controls
- Effects (wipes)
- Timelines

Players

The developer loads the needed media into the appropriate player—for example, graphics are loaded into the sprite player, and sounds are loaded into the sound player. Sprites can consist of single graphics or multiple graphics that play like an animated GIF image. The media elements are then controlled individually, much the same way they are on a web page.

Other players include paths. Players, such as graphics or text, can be caused to move along a path from one place to another. Controls, including slider bars, can be used and then linked to control other elements on the screen. Moving a slider bar, for instance, could give you control over the position of a graphic on the screen.

You can also use effects that create wipes and fades. Note that Internet Explorer 4 works with almost all of the available wipes, while Netscape 4 can support only some of them.

Unlike some other multimedia development programs, the timeline is merely another player that can be used. Other players' actions can be coordinated using the timeline so as to create stage-based storytelling. This object (or player-based) way of development more closely mimics the nature of the web, where each element is designated and loaded separately. Not every page you create will be timeline-based, so why make this feature the center of your program? Sometimes you may just want to build an animated navigation bar.

Players are controlled by three main areas: data, properties, and handlers.

Data: The media are selected and imported using the Data dialog boxes. Multiple graphics may be imported at one time. Other players allow different items to be defined in the Data dialog boxes. The Real Audio player asks for a URL, for instance, while the timeline asks you to place other players on its sequencer.

Properties: Properties help control the layout of the players on the screen. The Properties dialog box in many ways resembles the functions of CSS-P. It can be used to establish position, visibility, opacity, preloading, draggability, and scrolling characteristics. The Properties window gives you pixel-perfect control over layout.

Handlers: Handlers resemble the event models for the version 4.0 browsers. They cause certain players to respond when the user does something. If a user runs the mouse over a sprite, a handler may cause another sprite to appear. Alternatively, the sprite may appear only if something else has been done first. Other triggering events include system events, such as pages loading or keyboard input. Interactor lets you add "conditionals" to further control your work. By keeping away from the complexity of multimedia scripting languages, such as Macromedia's Lingo, Interactor has managed to retain 95% of Director's functionality in an environment that more closely resembles the web.

Publishing

The strength of Interactor derives from its ability to publish to plug-in format, Active X control, Java, or the two varieties of Dynamic HTML. This publishing can sometimes be less than intuitive. Although the associated media files reside in the same directory as the HTML file, it would be nice to have them in a separate media directory. The JavaScript files must be loaded to the server along with the HTML and media files. Publishing should be easy if you are familiar with external JavaScript files.

Incorporating Mbedlets into a Web Page

Interactor is not a program that you would use to create entire web pages. The Dynamic HTML, Java, or plug-in format multimedia that it produces tend to occupy their own areas of the web page within a definite area. To have these mbedlets interact with the rest of the web page, you must edit the code. The code generated by Interactor can be somewhat hard to understand and modify. It is therefore best to keep the mbedlets as separate areas and build the rest of the page around them.

Conclusion

mBed Interactor gives you the ability to work around the limitations and incompatibilities of the different browsers by delivering what is best for each user. It achieves this effect within an intuitive authoring environment that does not have much of the needless complexity of Macromedia's Director/Shockwave. The authoring process closely resembles the web, in that you manipulate each object independently. It is the only currently available tool that delivers on the promise of Dynamic HTML in a true drag-and-drop authoring environment.

MACROMEDIA DREAMWEAVER

Dreamweaver is best thought of as a Visual Dynamic HTML development tool. It is not a true authoring environment or just an editor. Instead, it lies somewhere in between the two extremes and draws some of the best functions from both. I worked on the original beta team for this product. In fact, the first Dynamic HTML project I ever worked on, "Robots," is featured on the back of the box.

Let's talk about the interface (Figure A-2). Dreamweaver consists of a number of floating palettes around a central work area. The main work area is a WYSIWYG area called the Docu-

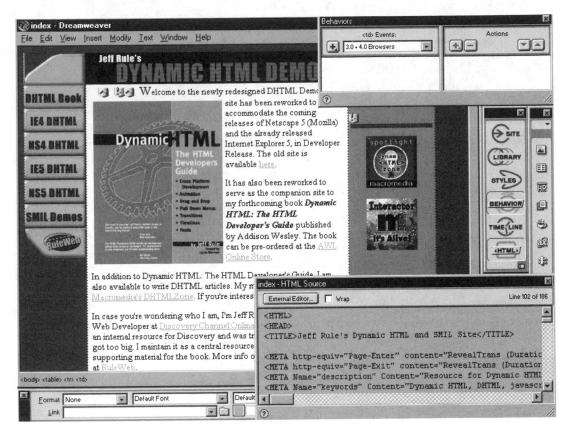

FIGURE A-2. Macromedia Dreamweaver interface

ment Window, where the elements can be dragged around the screen to reposition them. The floating palettes help you control the positioned elements in the main window.

Palettes

A variety of palettes are available in Dreamweaver.

Object: Icons for images, tables, forms, and, of course, Shockwave can be dragged from the Object palette into the Document Window. These icons can then be repositioned around the screen.

Site Window: The Site Window allows you to FTP to remote sites.

Library: The Library palette allows you to store objects that are reused in the project, much like the Library in Authorware.

Styles: The Styles palette acts as a storage area for CSS. With larger projects, you may find it indispensable. The ability to create one style and then reuse it from this area is much easier than cutting and pasting styles repeatedly.

Properties: The Properties inspector gives you access to all properties of an object.

Behaviors: The Behaviors inspector gives you a pull-down menu for all the events from the Internet Explorer 4.0 and Netscape 4.0 DOMs. You can forget having to remember syntax; you simply pick from the menu, and Dreamweaver writes cross-platform code for the particular event for you. Dreamweaver offers built-in actions such as checking plug-ins, swapping images, showing or hiding layers and images, changing attributes, and jumping to favorite places on the timeline.

What would a Macromedia product be without a Director/Flash-style timeline? The timeline allows actions to take place over time. As discussed in Chapter 10, it can transform the web into a stage where stories occur over time. Timelines give the web a fourth dimension, making it much more like CD-ROM.

RoundTrip HTML Editing

While WYSIWYG editors are nice, you inevitably have to tweak the source code. Dreamweaver has handled this issue in two ways. First, the source code is always available to be edited in a small window. There is no need to change modes. Changes made to the code show up in real time in the WYSIWYG window. Second, RoundTrip allows you to export your code to Homesite 3.0 on the PC or BBEdit on the Macintosh. Using these editors, you can change the code and send it back to Dreamweaver, where it will be updated. RoundTrip is the kind of tool that shows Macromedia's true understanding of how web programming is done. The fact that Dreamweaver also puts out legible code is a great benefit.

Dreamweaver 1.2 offers a number of nice advances over the initial release. The most recent release allows you to import tables and output the result in CSS, and vice versa. This nice conversion tool even works on nested tables and very complex tables.

All in all, Dreamweaver is an exceptional tool. Macromedia has built a tool that matches the way real developers work and that adjusts itself to several skill levels. Despite its high price ($299), Dreamweaver is a must-have tool for the professional developer.

For more definitions, see Webopedia provided by Internet.com (http://webopedia.internet.com).

Active X A proprietary technology owned by Microsoft that grew out of Object Linking and Embedding (OLE). Microsoft uses Active X and Component Object Model (COM) to allow distributed application development across networks, such as the Internet. You will generally encounter Active X in the form of a web-based technology that allows small applications to be embedded in web pages or that acts similarly to Netscape plug-ins.

Active X multimedia controls Active X controls that are part of Microsoft's Internet Explorer 4.0 and include the Sequencer, Path, Sprite, and Structured Graphics controls. Unlike normal Active X controls, the multimedia controls are part of the browser and do not need to be downloaded.

aliased Graphics that appear to have a jagged edge when viewed closely because the resolution of the monitor is not sufficiently high to mask the individual pixels. Many graphics programs allow you to soften these harsh edges by using anti-aliasing.

Allaire Cold Fusion A program that allows database information to be presented directly in a web page by using a script-like language. It runs on Sun and Windows NT systems.

animated GIF image A multiframe image produced with a GIF animation tool. It can play once or as a loop. The image is not interactive or controllable by the user.

animation A still image that can be moved around the screen on a certain path or a series of images that are presented rapidly to present the illusion of continuous motion.

array In programming, a series of objects all of which are the same type. Each object in the array is called an array element. Storing objects in an array allows you to keep like objects conveniently in one place to be used as needed.

browser detection A method of presenting specific information to users of a particular browser. This technique allows you to work around browser incompatibilities or to take advantage of particular features of a certain browser.

Cascading Style Sheets (CSS) A technique that works with HTML to give developers more control over the layout of web pages. CSS allows for pixel-perfect positioning of page elements as well as layering.

channel A general term for content delivered using push technology, such as Microsoft Channels in Internet Explorer 4 or Netcaster in Netscape Communicator.

Channel Definition Format (CDF) A format that describes information to be pushed to users using channels. Microsoft, which initially developed the standard, has submitted it to the World Wide Web Consortium for standards consideration. Companies such as Pointcast and WebTV are already using the CDF standard.

Character Shape Player (CSP) A technology built into Netscape Communicator that interprets downloadable fonts and displays them in the browser.

Document Object Model (DOM) A model that defines how HTML objects (such as graphics and text) are exposed to the scripting language. The DOM controls how the scripting language is used to change attributes such as color or the choice of graphic image.

drag and drop A technique whereby clicking and holding down the mouse button allows objects to be moved around the screen. Releasing the mouse button causes the object to stop moving with the mouse. This technique is widely used in operating systems such as Windows and the Macintosh operating system. It can be duplicated for the web using DHTML.

dynamic filters In Microsoft Internet Explorer 4.0+, a filter that can be applied to objects, such as graphics, in real time.

Dynamic HTML (DHTML) A combination of scripting, Cascading Style Sheets, and the Document Object Model that allows web pages to be dynamically changed in real time. This language makes techniques such as animation and drag and drop possible on a web page. Microsoft and Netscape support conflicting versions of Dynamic HTML in their version 4 browsers.

Dynamic HTML behavior An unapproved extension to Cascading Style Sheets 2 (CSS2). A web developer can separate Dynamic HTML code from HTML code by applying the Dynamic HTML behavior to an object on the screen. The behavior is stored in an external file and can be applied to many different objects on the screen.

dynamic property A property that allows CSS to react to the environmental conditions in which it is being displayed. For example, the font size might vary with a change in the screen size.

ECMAScript A general-purpose, cross-platform programming language derived from JavaScript. Netscape turned control of JavaScript over to ECMA, a Europe-based industry association that is dedicated to the standardization of information and communication systems, so as to make JavaScript a universal standard.

event An action taken by either the user or the browser. Events include such actions as mouse clicks or page loading.

filter A script that allows some object to be manipulated in a pre-defined mathematical way. In this book, filters apply to the manipulation of graphical images via scripting.

font A design for a set of characters. Fonts describe the look and feel of how letters appear on the screen. A font is the combination of typeface and other qualities, such as size, pitch, and spacing.

font definition file The format in which downloadable fonts for Netscape Communicator 4 are described. Fonts are stored in a Portable Font Resource (PFR) file.

Hypertext Markup Language (HTML) The language used to describe the layout of web pages.

Java An object-oriented, high-level programming language for the web. Originally developed by Sun Microsystems for hand-held devices, Java was moved to the web in 1995. Although it was originally envisioned as a cross-platform programming language using Java Virtual Machine for playback, the technology has encountered performance and compatibility problems.

JavaScript The original scripting language that was included in Netscape 2.0. Although it shares many of the features and structures of the full Java language, JavaScript was developed independently by Netscape. Programs written in this language can interact with HTML source code, enabling web authors to add interactivity to their web pages.

layering Overlapping HTML objects via Cascading Style Sheets. An example would be text sitting on top of a graphic.

Macromedia Backstage A visual web-page development environment that permits the integration of database content using a scripting language (much like Allaire Cold Fusion).

mouseover An event that occurs when the user moves the mouse pointer over an object. Such events are used to trigger scripting.

Netcaster A part of Netscape Communicator 4.0 that acts as the receiver for push content delivered in Netscape's push format.

object detection Much like browser detection, a technique that allows the developer to find out if the user's browser supports certain features. Once this determination is made, the content can be customized so as to best fit the user's browser.

path animation An animation created when an object—usually a graphic—is moved along a path created by a series of points.

point-to-point animation An animation that occurs on a straight line between two points.

Portable Font Resource (PFR) The file format for downloadable fonts for Netscape Communicator 4.0+.

programming language A set of rules for telling a computer how to perform certain tasks. High-level programming languages include Java, C++, BASIC, and JavaScript.

push technology Technology whereby information is downloaded to the user's machine without an active request by the user. Users generally subscribe to a push technology service, and the subscription information is downloaded based on a certain schedule. Normal web browsing is based on a pull model, in which the user requests the information and then it is downloaded.

raster graphic Also known as a bit-mapped graphic. Raster graphics consist of individual bits that are represented by pixels on the screen. Typical formats include BMP, JPG, GIF, and PICT.

rollover An event that occurs when an HTML object changes its appearance as the mouse moves over it. Such events are often used to change graphics when the user rolls the mouse pointer over it.

scripting language A simple programming language that allows you to control some element of a program. JavaScript is a scripting language.

Sequencer control One of the Active X multimedia controls included with Internet Explorer 4.0. It allows certain events to be triggered on a timeline.

Shockwave A widely distributed plug-in/Active X technology from Macromedia. It allows browsers that have the Shockwave plug-in or Active X control to display multimedia content in the browser window. Macromedia offers several content creation tools that are compatible with Shockwave, including Director, Flash, and Authorware. Shockwave is limited by its need for a plug-in or Active X control.

Sprite control One of the Active X multimedia controls included with Internet Explorer 4.0. It permits the creation of multi-layer graphics that can be manipulated by the user. In practice, this control behaves like a controllable animated GIF image.

static filter A filter used with Internet Explorer 4.0. Generally applied to text or graphics, it performs a mathematical calculation on the object that usually produces a visual result, such as a glow effect or a drop shadow.

Structured Graphics control An Active X control built into Internet Explorer 4.0 that is used to display vector graphics.

timeline A series of events that happen sequentially over time. A timeline is used in JavaScript to control a number of events that change the web page over time.

transitions Visual effects that smooth the change from one visual element to another. Examples include fades and wipes.

VBScript A scripting language based on Microsoft's Visual Basic. This language is supported by Microsoft Internet Explorer only and has much the same functionality as JavaScript.

vector graphic A graphic that is based on points and mathematical calculations. A curved line is represented by two points and a mathematical description of the arc between them. In contrast, a raster graphic describes all the points on the arc.

Web Embedding Font Tool (WEFT) A tool provided by Microsoft that prepares fonts for downloading over the Internet into Internet Explorer 4.0+.

webtop A term used by Netscape to describe a computer's graphical desktop, which is built with information downloaded and updated over the web.

XML (Extensible Markup Language) A language that enables designers to create customized tags that provide functionality not ordinarily available with HTML. The new tags help to define elements not covered in HTML. The browser must understand these elements or they will be ignored.

XSL (Extensible Stylesheet Language) A language for expressing style sheets, which are used to format XML documents. The relationship between XSL and XML is similar to the relationship between CSS and HTML.

index

Note: Page numbers in **boldface** indicate glossary definitions.

Addison-Wesley Computer and Engineering Publishing Group

How to Interact with Us

1. Visit our Web site

http://www.awl.com/cseng

When you think you've read enough, there's always more content for you at Addison-Wesley's web site. Our web site contains a directory of complete product information including:

- Chapters
- Exclusive author interviews
- Links to authors' pages
- Tables of contents
- Source code

You can also discover what tradeshows and conferences Addison-Wesley will be attending, read what others are saying about our titles, and find out where and when you can meet our authors and have them sign your book.

2. Subscribe to Our Email Mailing Lists

Subscribe to our electronic mailing lists and be the first to know when new books are publishing. Here's how it works: Sign up for our electronic mailing at **http://www.awl.com/cseng/mailinglists.html**. Just select the subject areas that interest you and you will receive notification via email when we publish a book in that area.

3. Contact Us via Email

cepubprof@awl.com
Ask general questions about our books.
Sign up for our electronic mailing lists.
Submit corrections for our web site.

bexpress@awl.com
Request an Addison-Wesley catalog.
Get answers to questions regarding your order or our products.

innovations@awl.com
Request a current Innovations Newsletter.

webmaster@awl.com
Send comments about our web site.

cepubeditors@awl.com
Submit a book proposal.
Send errata for an Addison-Wesley book.

cepubpublicity@awl.com
Request a review copy for a member of the media interested in reviewing new Addison-Wesley titles.

We encourage you to patronize the many fine retailers who stock Addison-Wesley titles. Visit our online directory to find stores near you or visit our online store: **http://store.awl.com/** or call **800-824-7799**.

Addison Wesley Longman
Computer and Engineering Publishing Group
One Jacob Way, Reading, Massachusetts 01867 USA
TEL 781-944-3700 • FAX 781-942-3076